## PART 1

# INTRODUCTION

# & HISTORY

# OF THE

# TRAMWAY SYSTEM

In compiling this book I have received a great deal of invaluable help and encouragement, from the following: Peter Davey for allowing me to see and photograph his collection of Bristol Tram memorabilia, Mike Tozer, and Janet and Derek Fisher for providing so many of the interesting historical photographs, Don Goddard for his help in reading and correcting the proof, to all of them I wish to record my sincere thanks. Many thanks are also given to my wife Doreen for her encouragement, help and patience in checking over the words written and correcting the many mistakes.

*May 1995*                                                                 *I.S. Bishop*

DEDICATED TO ZOE
OUR FIRST GRANDCHILD

By the same author: OLDLAND the VILLAGE and the PARISH

ISBN 09526490.0.4

Published by:
I.S. Bishop, 32 Henfield Crescent,
Oldland Common, Bristol. BS15 6SF

Printed by:
Adlard Print & Typesetting Services,
The Old School, The Green,
Ruddington, Notts NG11 6HH

# "THE CITY AND KINGSWOOD LINE"

## PREFACE

During the 1930's a small band of tram enthusiasts spent many hours touring Bristol, photographing the electric traction cars which were then quite numerous in the streets of our city. Fortunately the pictures of H.B. Priestly, S. Miles Davey, W.A. Camwell and others have survived, and having been collected by the author and others, are grouped together in this book to give the reader an insight into the style of public transport in this city during the full period of almost forty-six years that the electric trams operated, and served Bristol and the surrounding districts so well.

The 14 October 1895 saw the inauguration of the first electric tram service in Bristol, with the opening of the line from Old Market to Kingswood. Some forty-six years later the very last passenger carrying tram to operate in Bristol was working the same route when its motive power was brought to a sudden and unexpected end as a result of hostile enemy action. In compiling this book I have attempted to set out the background story of Bristol's Trams, how they came into existence, and how they contributed to the growth of public transport, whilst at the same time concentrating on the two lines which form the basis of the pictorial story. The pictures used have been chosen so that the reader can take an imaginary tram journey from Hanham to Old Market and on out to Knowle, with the return journey from the Tramway Centre to Kingswood. Many of Bristol's Trams can be individually seen in the book as they went about their work, whilst the last section deals with their unfortunate demise.

This book is not only of great local interest, it will also appeal to all those who are fascinated by the urban electric trams once so common in all major towns and cities in the first half of this century, particularly those who will recall/appreciate the fact that Bristol had in the 1920's and 1930's the largest fleet of open-top trams in the whole country. History may well repeat itself, and perhaps in the not too distant future Bristol may again, as have other cities, have trams conveying the public through the present motor crowded streets.

# INTRODUCTION

As towns and cities grew larger and larger during their medieval expansion to a size recognisable today, many if not most of the inhabitants tended to confine their life's activities to a relatively small area of their home town. The reason for this was in the main brought about by the enormous difficulty in simply getting around. Whilst the well off could and did ride around in their own carriage, or on their own horse, there was no such luxury for the majority, they just had to walk.

Such a situation continued in Bristol, which ranked in size and stature as the second city in the land, until the late eighteenth century when during 1784 the very first hackney carriages appeared on the streets. Around thirty such horse-drawn vehicles began to operate, and no doubt they were used by those who were not quite wealthy enough to own their own carriage, but considered themselves to be too important to walk. For the majority of the citizens of Bristol life went on in very much the same way, and they continued to walk where ever they needed to go.

Over the next two to three generations, changes were occurring in the city, with the rich moving out into the country away from the stench of the urban areas, plus the need for improved housing and sanitation, and the ability for the majority of the citizens to move beyond their previous confines of the overcrowded narrow streets.

With factories growing to combine that which had previously been carried out in small workshops or even homes, and with the need to bring an ever increasing workforce to the factory gates, thoughts began to turn to the revolutionary idea of having some form of organised **public transport.**

Around 1865, some five years after George Train an American had opened Britain's first tramway in Birkenhead, a number of London based speculators decided to promote in Parliament the North Somerset Railway Bill, to include plans for the construction of no less than seven horse-drawn tramway routes into Bristol. Not for the last time, the City Council decided that as they had not thought up the idea, it would be totally wrong for any profits which might arise from such a venture, to go to London instead of staying in Bristol. They therefore opposed the proposal on the grounds that such a tramway system should be in the hands of, and controlled by, local people. Beyond that, they do not appear to have taken any steps to promote or back such a system by a local consortium.

This inevitably led to delays, and whilst other cities and towns developed their own tramway systems, Bristol continued to be mistrustful of schemes which might make money. Eventually Bristol Corporation stirred from its archaic and timid ideas of being merchant venturers, and in 1871 obtained powers which would enable it to borrow £14,000 to have a tramway constructed. The plans laid before Parliament was for the construction of two unconnected lines, one running from Old Market to St. George, the other from Colston Street to Blackboy Hill.

Despite the years of delay, the whole proposal had not been properly thought through, and by the time that the necessary Act of Parliament received the Royal Assent, the cost of construction had risen so much that the Corporation had only sufficient funds for the second line to be constructed.

Worse was yet to follow as no company had been formed to run the tramway, and surprisingly the Corporation had not thought of seeking such powers when the Bill was going through Parliament.

Eventually in 1874 the Bristol Tramways Company Ltd. was formed, and with the necessary finances secured, all seemed set for trams to be ordered and the system to be commissioned by mid summer, to include not only the original line to St. George, but also a line to Eastville as well as a connecting link from Old Market to the top of Colston Street. There was however a potential problem that had completely slipped the Corporation's mind, no one had considered the possibility that opposition might come from some if not all of the well to do citizens of this fair City. Before the first tram could be ordered, residents of the fashionable Clifton terraces raised objections, not so much against the tram, it could after all be used to their advantage to ease their journey home back up the hill. What troubled these homely wealthy Cliftonians was what the tram might bring in to their environment, an invasion of commoners, tradesmen, artisans, but worst of all perhaps their noisy children; people of the working class who could dirty and generally spoil the district's amenities, not to say their homes and gardens. The call to sweep the opposition to victory, was taken up by the church and temperance societies, the latter fearing that the introduction of cheap public transport in the form of these new-fangled trams would simply have the effect of bringing more and more sinners into the area of respectability.

Such opposition to the trams was not confined to just Clifton. Understandably, the introduction of anything new always brings in its wake, fears that the established way of life will change, and change for the worse. In St. George and along the main roads of Lawrence Hill, local shopkeepers and numerous stall traders saw the introduction of the tram as a threat to their own livelihoods, because they only considered the possibility that the trams would take people away to the big shops in the city centre, rather than the possibility that the trams would also bring new customers in from outside of the locality. Wherever the opposition came from, it united together to try and block the Bill from going through Parliament, and in doing so it surprised and dismayed the City Council and their backers. Fortunately this was the enlightened age of Victorian progress determined to push this country into the twentieth century, and Parliament allowed the Act to go through.

Twelve months had been lost whilst the arguments against the tramway systems had been considered, during which time the line from Colston Street to Blackboy Hill had lain unused, and subjected to the abuse of the other road traffic, and lack of maintenance. Eventually, in July 1875, the first tram car which had been built in Leamington Spa, arrived at Temple Meads Station. From there it was conveyed by cart to the top of Colston Street, and placed upon the awaiting rails. Two horses were attached, and with James C. Robinson the company manager at the control, the tram was taken to Redland and back. Adjustments were needed to improve the track, and finish the depot for the cars and the stables for the horses. After this work was carried out, the tramway was officially opened at noon on Monday 9th August 1875.

December of that year saw the line extended around the sharp curve at Perry Road, down the hill to the Drawbridge. With the Redland line proving to be popular and financially successful, further work was carried out laying track around the city, so that by June 18765 the line from Old Market to Eastville was opened. These two independent lines did not stay separated for long, the navvies completing the connecting line from the Drawbridge (Centre) to the Horsefair, and on through Broadmead and Lower Castle Street to Old Market, by September 1876.

Trams were regarded as a wonderful invention, providing relatively inexpensive travel to the bulk of the citizens for the very first time. Each horse-drawn tram had an overall length of seventeen feet, which enabled no less than 32 people to sit down on benches contained on two decks. (In the form of a wooden "knifeboard" on the top deck, and longitudinal cushioned benches in the lower saloon). In addition, there could be anything up to 30 people standing, with the whole vehicle and weight being pulled by just two horses. Although there was, in the early stages, a certain amount of curiosity with these new-fangled carriages, the records show that during the first month of operation, which was of course restricted to the Redland line, no fewer than 115,000 passengers were carried, while the tram cars collectively covered 5,887 miles.

With enthusiasm born from the great desire to succeed, the company pushed on with further extensions, this time concentrating on branching the Old Market/Eastville line at Holy Trinity Church, on through Lawrence Hill, Redfield to St. George, opening the line in October 1876. The legal authority to open this line came in an Act of Parliament which confirmed certain provisional Orders made by the Board of Trade under The Tramways Act 1870, relating to the Bristol and Eastern

District Tramways, having received the Royal Assent on the 2nd August 1875. In this Act the Company was empowered to construct a line one mile one furlong and one chain in length starting from a point opposite Trinity Street, through Clarence Road and Lawrence Hill, on through the areas of Moorfields and Redfield to a point opposite the *Fire Engine* public house. That particular section was identified as Tramway No.3 by the Act, whereas Tramway No.4 is identified as a tramway, five furlongs six chains fifty links in length, wholly situated in the parish of St. George, commencing at the point of termination of Tramway No.3, and passing thence in an easterly direction along the public highway from Lawrence Hill to St. George, and terminating at a point in the said public highway seventeen yards or thereabouts east of the entrance to the *World's End* public house.

At the *World's End*, passengers wishing to continue on to Kingswood would have to transfer to a horse-bus service, whilst those on route to Hanham would have had to disembark at the St. George Fountain.

Within the next four years, the Company had opened lines to Hotwells, Totterdown, and Bedminster, but not to Kingswood or Hanham.

As the years rolls by, the initial enthusiasm of accepting this marvellous pioneering mode of public transport as being the wonder of the age, gave way to the scepticism that things could be better. Although the Tramway Company had endeavoured to plan these routes over the low level areas of the City, there are simply not that many ways you can go from one part of Bristol to another before encountering a hill of some description. Any hill would add to the strain of the two horses hauling the car, and thus at the very least, the speed of the tram car would be seriously reduced. Where steeper inclines were encountered, the two horses attached to the tram would not be able to cope on their own, and thus it was necessary to add trace horses. This meant, for example, that on the route to Hotwells, to get a fully-laden tram up the short hill from the Centre to Deanery Road, required the combined strength of no less than five horses. In addition there was the problem of hills which although not too steep were none the less both long and arduous, resulting in the need to periodically replace tired horses with fresh ones. All of this meant that the Company had to employ many more horses than might have been expected, and that there had to be at numerous strategic points around the City, a number of trace and fresh horses waiting their turn to keep the trams running. Needless to say this did not go down very well with other road users who saw these extra horses as simply taking up valuable road space, and once past their own vehicles were held up by the heaving and the plodding of the Company horses.

From the horses point of view, its working day was probably restricted to about one quarter of the tram crew, and certainly no more than four hours were worked in any twenty-four hour period. To cover its fleet of about 70 tram cars, the Company needed to employ 300 horses, at a cost of around 9d (4p) per mile, plus numerous stable lads, farriers and ostlers.

As a result of the difficulties, the inventive Victorians were continually looking at ways of improving the system not only for the benefit of the fare paying passengers, but also for the shareholders in the form of increased profits. All around them were the ever expanding railways, connecting towns and villages by steam hauled locomotives, and thus it seemed quite natural for the tramway engineers to see how such locomotion could be harnessed for their needs.

Bristol, as so often happens, was somewhat lagging behind these initiatives, as well as being rather cautious not to become too adventurous or pioneering. It was therefore a rather happy coincidence when, in 1877, the Tramway Company discovered the fact that a local engineering company, Messrs. Fox & Walker, were in the process of building six steam tram engines for the French town of Rouen, and that Fox & Walker would be prepared to try out one of these engines on the Tramway Company's rails. Because no one was sure of the effect that these engines would have on horses and/or passengers, it was decided that the first live trial would take place during the early hours of the 4th December 1877, when the steam engine pulling a horse car tram, would travel from Eastville to Redland. Everything appears to have gone quite well, until the vehicles reached the tight "U" turn at the top of Colston Street, a turn which the steam engine was just unable to negotiate. The journey to Redland had therefore to be abandoned, and both vehicles were taken to the depot at St. George. Although changes were made to the track to try and make the Perry Road/Colston Street turn easier to negotiate, further problems existed the following night, and within days the engine together with the other five were on their way to Rouen.

Almost three years were to pass before Bristol saw steam hauled trams on its roads again, when it was decided to invest in seven engines on a year's contract to be used on the line which ran from the Horsefair to Horfield. The inaugural run, with due display and ceremony, and a certain amount of steam, smoke, and much clanking left the Horsefair at 1 p.m. on the 18th November 1880. As would be expected only invited guests were allowed in the car., whilst the steam engine was under the anxious control of the company's resident engineer Clifton Robinson. All went well and soon the public were allowed to ride behind the power of steam on the open roads of north-east Bristol.

The steam engines were required by law to have all of their working/moving parts covered, and thus not visible to the public. This resulted in the engines having a box like structure, with windows, and a large pipe chimney which folded back horizontally over the roof of the engine box, which was capable of being connected to a chimney pipe fitted to the trailer. The trailers were all old horse-drawn trams which had been specially adapted with a canopy over the open top deck. The chimney pipe ran vertically up the top front from an elbow fitting, taking the hot choking smoke up from the engine over the canopy of the trailer. Whilst the passengers on the top deck were still exposed to the elements, they were at least (in theory) kept from the worst of the discomforts from the soot and smoke produced by the engine.

The power produced by these engines meant that no longer would the hills of Bristol create the problems they gave to the horse drawn trams, and the engineers soon had ideas to extend the use of steam to cover other routes. However, the steam engines brought with them their own problems inasmuch as they were noisy, dirty and smelly. Horses unused to such noise would bolt away as far as their legs would take them shedding as they went, their load and pedestrians in all directions. Some dogs would bark, whilst others ran away in fright, little children were left clutching at their mother's skirt in the hope that the dragons would not see them, whilst older children taunted them with their own bravado. Adults, particularly those who either lived or were shopkeepers along the route, complained of the smoke and smell which invaded their premises, as well as the soot which left a black film on everything it settled on.

The experiment lasted almost a full year, but with public opinion firmly against the use of steam engines on the streets of Bristol, the locomotives were withdrawn so that by the 4 November 1881 they were left to fade into being no more than a memory.

During most of the time that the experiment into steam lasted, the bulk of the lines in and around Bristol were isolated from each other, and it was not until April 1881 that the major routes were linked by connecting the Old Market terminus with the Drawbridge on what was to become known as the Tramway Centre.

Although in years to come it would be possible to catch a tram at Hanham and go all the way to the *Red Lion* at Knowle, prior to April 1881 this would have been physically impossible as apart from the fact that Hanham was still not on the system, there was in addition no track between Tower Hill and Bristol Bridge. Whenever it was necessary to transfer cars between the depot at Eastville, and the Totterdown (Three Lamps) line, the tram cars would have to be pulled off the track at Tower Hill and dragged over the cobblestones through Bath Street to Bristol Bridge where it could regain the tracks leading through Victoria Street and on to the Three Lamps. The line to Knowle was not to be completed for another 17 years.

1) Horse drawn tram 122 together with an unidentified tram wait at the centre, around 1890, before continuing with their respective journeys. With the horses producing their own pollution there was always plenty of work to do for the man with the broom!

2) Car 141 as it was originally delivered as a Director's Inspection vehicle. It was rebuilt as a standard passenger tram in 1908.

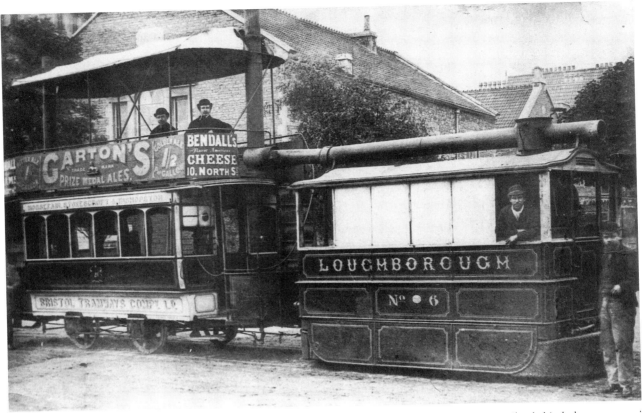

3) The only covered tram to run in Bristol was this converted horse tram which was fitted out as a trailer behind the steam engine Loughborough Nº.6. Captured here on film standing outside Horfield Methodist Church during 1881, this engine was one of seven locomotives supplied by Hughes Locomotive & Tramway Company.

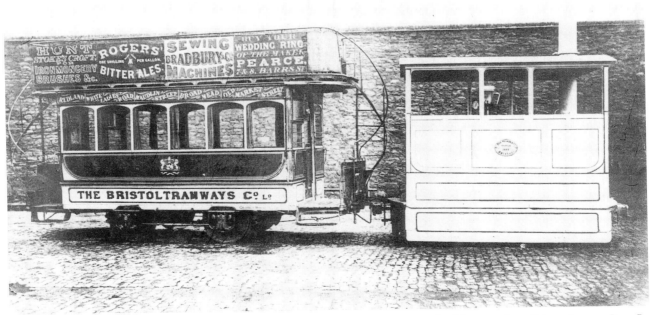

4) During the steam trials the company used this smaller locomotive so that it could negotiate the tight curve from Colston Street to Perry Road on the Old Market to Redland Route. Built in 1877 by the Bristol locomotive manufacturers Fox Walker & Co. painted all white, this vehicle distinguished itself during the trials but still had trouble with the curve.

5) Construction of the overhead wires meant that a special telescopic horse drawn tower wagon needed to be constructed complete with a turn table at the top of the tower. Pictured here during 1899 in the Bath Road along from the Three Lamps junction, the men's trust in the horse was paramount!

# ELECTRIFICATION

Having experimented with horse power and steam power, and having found problems and inconvenience with both, the tramway engineers considered other sources of power including electricity. In the early years of the last decade of the nineteenth century electric motors were beginning to be used to move trams around relatively short routes, such as a two mile run in Blackpool, whilst in Leeds they pioneered the overhead wire systems with a swivel-head trolley pole to enable the tram motor to collect the supply of electricity.

During this period, the Bristol Tramways & Carriage Company had as its advisor James Clifton Robinson (later Sir James), a man of great energy and vision, and who had, until 1882, been the Company's General Manager. Mr Robinson had for many years studied tramway systems around the world, and had many pioneering ideas about the ability of electrical power to provide the energy and the flexibility needed to take the tramways into the twentieth century. His belief in the use of electricity was carried with an infectious enthusiasm which was to be spread to the directors of the Tramway Company, and before long the Board of Directors were very keen to introduce this new power source to the city's tramcars.

Over a number of years, the Tramway Company had gradually, by steady and continuous progress expanded the Bristol system so that by 1882 there existed extensive tramway routes which spread their connecting branches through the populous districts of the City, and its suburbs. Already the company employed around 500 men and boys, plus 800 horses to pull 100 tramcars, to carry some 15,000,000 passengers during the course of the year. Thus on average, every man, woman and child in Bristol during the early 1880's would have had one horse drawn tram journey per week. Each horse would on average have pulled 18,750 passengers, whilst each car would have conveyed 150,000 passengers per year.

As anyone who lives in Bristol will understand, that geographically, the City is not very favourably situated for a tramway system, especially one which has to rely on the power of horses to tow the tramcars around many difficult gradients, some of which are insurmountable however many horses you use. In fact there can be few towns or cities in the country the size of Bristol, where so many different, and sometimes difficult grades exist around all points of the compass, making the progress of the running tram, or the proposed route uneconomical. Thus there had been for a number of years, in the minds of the directors, strong reasons for finding a suitable alternative means of power, especially the use of some form of mechanical power. Thus when Mr. Robinson introduced the very favourable idea of using electric traction, after its proven capacity in hilly towns in American to work over steep gradients, the whole notion of introducing electric traction to Bristol was received with great fascination, and enthusiasm.

Electrical power was of course still very much in its infancy in the 1880/90's, particularly in this country, and thus there was obvious concern both in Parliament and elsewhere to ensure that the introduction and use of electricity in public places and for public transport was safe not only to the public but also to the employees of the tramway concern. Most of the tramway systems either completed or being planned in the Country were of an American design, and this was certainly true of the proposed Bristol scheme. Unfortunately in America there was a design fault which caused a major problem inasmuch as the people were receiving electric shocks from stray current coming from the overhead wires. There was therefore an understandable ground swell of objections to the electrification of the tramway system, and overhead wires in particular. Consideration to these matters needed to be debated in Parliament, and in due course they issued specific regulations controlling the operation of electric traction on the public highway.

This enabled the directors to push through their ideas for the electrification of the tramway system in Bristol, choosing the Kingswood line to be the most suitable for the first conversion, as it not only passed through newly developing suburbs, but encountered a number of hills, with severe gradients, before it reached its destination.

The proposed new tramway therefore had an important part to play in the development of tramway traction in this country in convincing public authorities, as well as the few tramway companies who still needed convincing, that the modern electric tramways offered great advantages without any disqualifying features. Although the Bristol scheme was not the first tramway of its class in Britain, it must rank with the epoch-making enterprise in tramway history. Although much work had already been done in Leeds, and at the South Staffordshire Tramway Company, neither had received anything like the attention given to the proposed Kingswood Line, thus indicating the turn of the tide in the public's acceptance of electric tramway traction. As claimed in the November 1895 edition of THE RAILWAY WORLD "nothing but unreasonable prejudice now stands in the way of progress"

# THE BRISTOL, ST. GEORGE & KINGSWOOD LINE

The extension of the tramway from the existing terminus at St. George to Kingswood involved the construction of around two miles of new track. At the time that the decision was taken to electrify the line, the existing section from Old Market to St. George had been laid with just horse drawn trams in mind, but with the intended introduction of heavier cars, and more frequent use, this whole section needed to be removed and replaced with heavy steel girder rails, on a substantial road bed. The contractors, British Thomson-Houston Ltd., were therefore faced with the difficulties of digging up the old track, and laying all new heavy duty track from Old Market through to Kingswood along four miles of densely crowded streets, with a constant movement of traffic which could not or should not be held up. At this time, the areas of both St. George and Kingswood were showing every sign of vigorous growth in population and trade, and this fact was heightened by the news that there was being built the first electric tramway in Bristol. The direct benefits arising from the proposed extension were soon to be seen, putting to an end for ever the isolation felt by people living away from the centre of the city, and giving impetus to the improved status such areas obtained from better means of easy communication. It also meant that for the first time in history, people could move out from the overcrowding so addicted to the nature of the inner city since medieval times. In addition it also gave people the opportunity of not having to live within easy walking distance of where they worked, the birth of the commuter was about to arrive.

The first steps taken to bring about the Kingswood extension occurred during 1891 when the first provisional order for carrying out the work was obtained. However until the modified regulations recommended by the joint committee of both Houses of Parliament concerning the operation of electric traction were known, the project remained as a paper exercise. In anticipation of the recommendations being approved, the Board of Directors commissioned James Clifton Robinson to prepare a report on the feasibility of constructing the electric line to Kingswood. Other means of tractive power had not been simply ignored, but it was quickly recognised that to work such a tortuous and heavily-graded system by horse power alone was out of the question; the lines being mostly single track, the cost of their equipment and operation by cable would have been so great as to render that method unprofitable, and extremely impractical. With steam and other methods of tramway haulage already in vogue in that country at that particular time, but rejected by both the BTCC directors and the public, there was literally just electricity left as the only means of power available to them. Thus having decided upon electric power, the next decision was the form of electricity, and whether the power was to be collected from underground conduit, or overhead wire. After a somewhat protracted and thorough enquiry the overhead wire system was considered to be the only one commercially possible.

The whole plan was then laid before the Corporation of Bristol, and the local authorities in St. George and Kingswood. Independent investigations were made on behalf of each body, and unanimous support for the scheme was forthcoming. This led to the next stage which was for the Company to promote an Act of Parliament.

However as with all things, matters did not go entirely to plan as the following excerpts from the 1894 editions of the magazine THE RAILWAY WORLD explains:-

JANUARY. At a meeting of the Sanitary Committee of the Town Council, on the 5th inst., the town clerk presented a long communication from the secretary of the Bristol Tramway Company, Mr. George White, in relation to the proposed electric tramways, setting forth the particulars of the bill which had been deposited for the ensuing session of Parliament. The main feature of the bill is the electric working of the St. George's and Kingswood lines, and the directors of the Tramway Company invited the Corporation officials to accompany them to Walsall, for the purpose of inspecting the system of the electric traction there. A sub committee of the Council will probably confer with the directors, and endeavour to arrive at agreements upon any disputed points before the bill is taken up by the Parliament committee. Some objection was expressed to the overhead wire system, but it was finally decided to inspect electric tramways elsewhere before entering into full discussion of the matter.

APRIL. A more striking instance of the injury that one or two short-sighted individuals may do to the best interests of a community than the opposition that is to be offered to the bill of the tramways company, providing for the installation of an electric tramway to Kingswood, would be difficult to find. The local authorities immediately concerned, after careful consideration, have given their sanction to the plans which had also received the unofficial approval of the entire community, and the company were expecting an easy victory for their bill. To the surprise of the company and the friends of the new system, two firms in West Street suddenly announced their intention of opposing the laying of the lines, on the grounds that the rails will be laid so near the footpath as to cause inconvenience to ordinary vehicular traffic, although as a matter of fact it appears that apparently an objection to the system of electric traction, very probably because they have no knowledge of mechanical traction, and regard the old system of horse traction as something infinitely superior to any new-fangled notions. A committee formed at St. George and Kingswood has taken the matter up, and the general public, who were looking forward impatiently to improve methods, have not been slow in expressing their opinion of the action of the frontagers, who are thus obstructing the plans of the company.

SEPTEMBER. The Tramway Company's Act received Royal Assent early in the month, and the company will lose no time in commencing the conversion of their lines for electric traction.

# ABRIDGED REPORT ON THE EXTENSION TO KINGSWOOD

The following is an abridged copy of the report prepared by J. Clifton Robinson to the Chairman and Directors of the Bristol Tramway and Carriage Company Limited, with regard to Bristol Tramways Extension.

*Ball's Bridge Dublin*
*December 1893*

*Gentlemen,*

*In submitting a Report on the question of introducing Electric Traction on the proposed Kingswood Extension and St. George Section of the Bristol Tramways, it may be convenient that I should first bring before you a sketch of the rise, progress, and present position of Electric Traction as applicable to Street Railway or Tramway purposes.*

There then follows twenty-five pages outlining the history of electric traction comparison between British and American lines, other lines in the country, descriptions of cars, and power houses, safety matters, speed of vehicles, and a host of other matters largely of a technical nature.

*I now turn to the practical part of my report, namely the proposal to apply electricity on the St. George and Kingswood Extension of your Company's system. Having been largely engaged in the early organisation and management of your Tramways, it is with great satisfaction I find myself commissioned to report on what will, I believe, prove the beginning of a further and very profitable development of the Bristol system. The tramway lines belonging to your Company cover in all, some 14 miles of street, the whole of them being at present worked by horse traction. As already mentioned, the operation of those lines indicates that every inhabitant of the district served makes 51 journeys by car yearly. According to the figures achieved elsewhere in the United Kingdom, this is a fairly satisfactory result, but when a comparison is made with the use of tramways in America, in cities of lesser importance than Bristol, it is clear that an immense field remains for cultivation by means of extensions between the city and its suburbs. But to enable the Company to exploit the necessary lines for creating that traffic and developing it, some less expensive method than horse traction must be sought, and this I am able with perfect confidence, to say has been found in the recent advance of electric power.*

*The extension of the tramway from its present terminus at St. George to Kingswood involves the construction of 1 mile 7 furlongs, or including single and double tracks, 2 miles 1 furlong and 7$^1/2$ chains of new line. At the present time horse cars run from Bristol Bridge to St. George, but in the proposal I am now to submit the city terminus of the extended line would preferably be at the city end of Old Market Street. The section to be operated by Electric Traction would thus present a total length of street tramway of about three miles four furlongs.*

*Both at St. George and Kingswood, there is every sign of vigorous growth in population and trade, and the history of Tramways has been written in vain if it is not now a fact so well established as to be incontrovertible, that the formation of such a communication at once stimulated the development and enhances the value of every district into which it extends.*

Other points were then made with regard to the construction of the line and the relationship of the utility companies that could be affected by the introduction of electric traction power. Finally the report finished:

1. *That electric traction presents a truly remarkable history in its speed of development.*

2. *That this development may be traced to two or three leading factors, such as its economy in working as opposed to horse or other modes of mechanical traction, its adaptability to all circumstances of great or small traffic, moderate or severe gradients, and city or suburban districts, and its special value in providing for out-lying suburbs where other methods of propulsion could not be financially successful.*

3. *That as regards Bristol, the case of the St. George and Kingswood extension offers an exceedingly favourable opportunity for making a beginning in the use of electro-motors, and that upon a very low and conservative view of traffic possibilities it shows a satisfactory return on the capital invested.*

*I have some confidence in pl.acing this report in the hands of your Board, being satisfied that if the proposal now brought forward be vigorously carried out, the public will greatly appreciate the opening up of the important district of Kingswood, and that, at no far distant date, the Corporation will suggest the extension of the use of Electric Traction to other districts of Bristol.*

*I have the honour to be, Gentlemen,*

*your obedient servant,*

J. CLIFTON ROBINSON.

# CONSTRUCTION OF ROUTE

The start of the route was at the western, or city end of Old Market with four sets of rails, with cross-overs to suit any traffic arrangement, bearing in mind that to start with there was still the need to accommodate existing horse drawn tram routes. The need to change over to a heavier rail, and a more solid foundation had therefore to be carried out with the least amount of disruption to the daily running of trams as possible.

Upon leaving Old Market in an easterly direction, the tracks narrowed to two, passing through West Street to Trinity Church where, after one-third of a mile from the starting point, the horse line to Eastville via Stapleton Road branched off to the left. The Kingswood line, still double tracked, then continued along Clarence Road to Lawrence Hill, crossing the South Wales branch of the Great Western Railway. Up to this point (about one-fifth of the 4 mile journey), the gradients are fairly easy, except for one short length to get the trams over the railway. However from this point on there is a basic climb of about 1 in 30 through Moorfields, Russel Town, and on through Church Road, Redfield, passing the *Fire Engine* public house where the track ceased to be independently doubled, to a double track which was occasionally interlaced. From here the gradient began to steepen, and having passed the *Don John's Cross* the trams were faced with about 220 yards of 1 in 15 to take them up to the fountain at St. George, and into Clouds Hill Road. From then on the trams encountered gradients of around 1 in 20 with the road continuing to rise up through Bell Hill Road and Two Mile Hill until it reached the Bristol/Kingswood boundary, some 300 feet above the starting point in Old Market. From here the line through Regent Street was relatively level, with the last half mile of the journey through High Street on a slightly descending gradient, to the terminus situated at the top of Hill Street.

The electricity required to operate the trams was produced by the Company at its own power station in Beaconsfield Road, St. George, the equipment being installed in what was originally their stables and car-shed. To house the engines, boilers, dynamos, electrical appliances and machinery as well as the electric tram cars, the engine and boiler houses needed to be re-roofed, and the car-sheds slightly extended, whilst at the same time the shed floor was considerably lowered so that sufficient headway could be achieved to accommodate the trolley standards. Two Lancashire boilers, thirty-feet long with mechanical stokers were installed, and these enabled three continuous current dynamos to each produce an out-put of 200 amperes at 550 volts, when working at 650 revolutions per minute. In addition there was a motor-generator which supplied current for accumulators, and for the lighting of the station.

From the power station, the electrical supply was sent out through the overhead trolley wires, returning through the track. Two complete trolley wires ran from end to end of the line to supply the necessary direct-current to cars running in opposite directions, and are held above the street by bracketed standards. Throughout Old Market Street and Lawrence Hill, they rise from the centre of the road, 30ft apart, with brackets on either side, and in the case of those erected in Old Market are surmounted alternately by electric arc lights. The others are erected along the southern side of the road, with a bracketed arm stretching across the road all the way through to Kingswood. The standards, which have been supplied by Messrs. Morris Tasker & Company of Philadelphia, are made in steel tubes of three lengths, which are over-lapped, and are shrunk together while hot. Over the base is passed a cast-iron sheath, which together with the pole is imbedded in concrete to a depth of 6ft. An armoured feeder was laid underground throughout the whole length of the line, connected every half-mile to a cast iron pillar, which contained switches and a lightning arrester between the feeder and the overhead wires.

The rolling stock initially consisted of 12 tram cars, each sufficiently powerful enough to pull an ordinary horse tram as a trailer. Each car was built by George F. Milne & Co., of Birkenhead being transported to Bristol by rail, and were probably unloaded at the Midland Railway's St. Philips depot, Midland Road. The trucks were of the American Peckham cantilever type, whilst the platforms were slightly longer than those on a horse drawn tram, so as to allow the driver to handle the controller in front of the stairs. Each car was fitted with a magnetic brake and a short-circuiting switch on both platforms to enable the motors to be used as a braking system. The cars, which were given the fleet numbers 86-97, were twenty-four feet long and five feet six inches wide, holding a twelve foot nine inch long body which could seat 18 persons inside, and 25 on the roof. The roof was nine foot six inches from rail level, with the six foot trolley-post being situated off centre half way along. Within the tram cars, there were two separate lighting systems employed simultaneously, the first came from the 'mains' and provided power for four lamps inside and one on top. The second system obtained electricity from accumulators and powered a second roof light, plus the head and destination lights at either end of the tram.

A final and interesting point should perhaps now be made of the employees who had to cope with many changes to their conditions of working during the 1890's. Quoting from a publication produced at the time:- *As regards the staff employed, it is not necessary to obtain skilled labour for traffic service, ordinary horse-car drivers being readily instructed in their duties as motor men, everything connected with the management and control of the cars being reduced to the utmost simplicity. It is worthy of note in connection with the electric traction that the cars can make an average mileage of 100 miles a day, without exceeding the Board of Trade limit; and this is about double the rate of speed which can be obtained with ordinary horse-car. Further, on special occasions, trailers for passengers may be attached to the motor cars and thus afford additional accommodation to the travelling public.*

6) This picture was probably taken in September 1895, when a number of trial runs were being carried out prior to the inauguration of public services. Almost certainly another orchestrated picture as spectators pose in front of the camera, and in front of this new vehicle. Note horse drawn tram just entering Old Market Street, behind the electric car.

7) Another trial run before the opening, car 92 again, no uniforms for driver under training. No advertisements. Somewhere between Old Market and St. George but exact location unknown.

8) The new electric service had been in operation for just over six months when Car 94 towing an old three windowed horse car (No.113) as a trailer, stopped in Old Market, near the junction with Capt. Carey's Lane. The majority of the passengers enjoy the summer sunshine sitting on the top deck, whilst the driver keeps his eye on the photographer. June 1896.

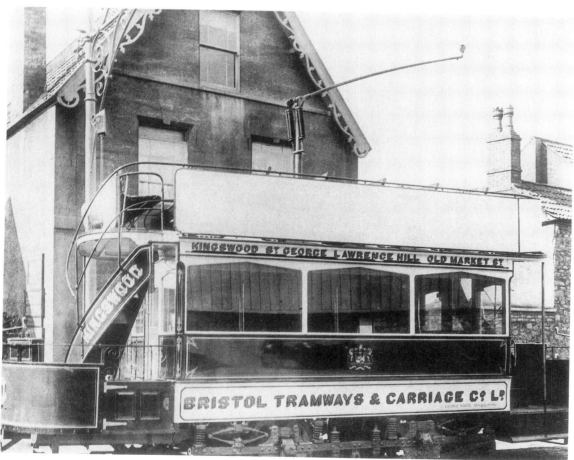

9) The exact location of this picture is not known. House behind is similar to those in Church Road, near to the Beaconsfield Road Depot, but the right-hand building does not seem to fit that particular location. The picture, of what is probably Tram No.90, clearly shows the width of the three windows, (four were fitted when the trams were rebuilt) the overhang of the platform, and the permanent route written above the ventilation panel. Note small solid half-door across the wrought iron balustrade, and the early design overhead troller arm. c.September 1895.

10) Two new electric cars numbered 89 and 92 have been carefully placed on the depot junction at St. George with the former tram on the spur leading into Beaconsfield Road. All the people have also been carefully posed by the photographer, no doubt as a publicity stunt to promote interest in the new system to start in the next few weeks. c.September 1895.

11) Another demonstration and publicity stunt, with car 89, and possibly car 92 together with its seven windowed horse tram trailer No.41 behind, in the Regent Street/High Street area of Kingswood. The top deck of the trailer is only available to be used by men, ladies will not be allowed upstairs on the grounds that there are no decency boards fitted. Young man with deer-stalker cap, (see front of group on left) also appears standing on the platform of tram 92 in the previous picture. Note open stairs and curtains at the windows. c.September 1895.

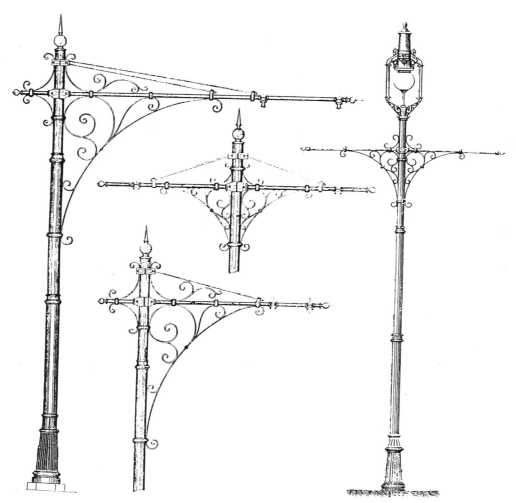

12) Types of trolley poles used when constructing the electric line to Kingswood

13) The great day has arrived, the electrified line has been given a clean bill of health by the Board of Trade, and now the line can be officially opened. This picture shows the pomp and ceremony, plus a huge public response to this event. The car nearest the camera is probably No.89 with William Butler (Chairman), George White (Managing Director), and Mr. Alderman Pethick (Bristol's High Sheriff) on board. All together eight decorated trams would leave Old Market at 12.30 p.m., and drive to Kingswood as part of the inaugural proceedings on that day, the 14 October 1895.

# THE INAUGURAL PROCEEDINGS

The work of up-grading the tracks, and the installation of the street poles and trolley wires caused much excitement and interest amongst the general public throughout 1894 and 1895, full of an eager anticipation for the first sight of the new fangled electric trams. Those who lived along the route were keen to see how the system would work, whether the new trams would be as clean and as quiet as forecast and whether they would enjoy riding these machines.

The Tramway Company not wishing to be exposed to possible ridicule if things did not go right first time, decided that discretion was the better part of valour, and accordingly arranged for the initial running trials to be carried out under cover of darkness. It was therefore with a certain amount of circumspection that the first tram left Beaconsfield Road Depot shortly after midnight in September 1895 to carry out a 'dry-run' in the comparative peace of the night. They may have got away with it if they had not overlooked the fact that as the trolley ran along the wire it quite frequently caused electric flashing, which was bright enough to momentarily light-up the bedrooms of the houses along the route, causing the good people of St. George to waken from their early slumbers. Realising that the Tramway Company was trying to steal a march on them, the neighbourhood was soon aroused, and despite the chill of the night, bedrooms windows were raised so that a glimpse of the first car could be seen. Knowing that in due course the tram would need to go back to the depot, many of the citizens remained looking out of their windows and/or front doors awaiting the return of this surreptitious tram-car. Never before or perhaps since has a Bristol tram-car been awaited by so many scantily-clad people. With the first trial run successfully carried out more followed, and with confidence growing the Company allowed trials and publicity runs to take place during day-light hours. Over the next month or so the whole length of the route was tested, with each journey being greeted with great enthusiasm.

By the end of September the trials had gone well enough for the system to be fully inspected by Majors Marindin and Cardew, both of the Royal Engineers, on behalf of the Board of Trade, and on the 2 October 1895, the Bristol Tramways & Carriage Co. Ltd., received official consent to operate the line by electric power.

The Company decided that the official day of opening the route would be Monday 14 October, and at 12.30 p.m. car number 89 carrying William Butler (Chairman), George White (Managing Director and later to become Sir George), Mr. Alderman Pethick (Bristol's High Sheriff) and numerous other distinguished guests, headed a procession of 8 decorated tram-cars equally filled with around a further 200 distinguished guests, left Old Market en route to Kingswood. Whilst it is not certain who drove the first car, it is known that the second car was driven by Mr. Clifton Robinson, who had with him the gentlemen of the Press, and councillors of St. George (then not part of the City of Bristol).

The journey of around four miles to Kingswood, was accomplished in about thirty minutes, with this new form of public transport eliciting from those, who were unlikely to frequent the system, expressions of the greatest praise and satisfaction. Once at the Kingswood terminus the 8 cars were drawn up in close order, and Mr. William Butler gave a short speech, declaring the line open. The distinguished guests then returned to their respective tram-cars, allowing the procession to return to the Beaconsfield Road Depot, where the guests were invited to inspect the power station, and the electrical plant and machinery. Having carried out their cursory inspection, the guests once again return to the tram-cars to be conveyed back to Old Market. From there they were taken by carriage to adjourn to the Grand Hotel, where luncheon was served in the Assembly Room to the accompaniment of an excellent selection of music played by the band of The Royal Artillery.

After the luncheon, Mr. William Butler rose to his feet, and proposed a toast to "The Queen" followed by a toast to the Bristol Corporation, and the District Councils of St. George and Kingswood. He then went on to give a speech setting out the reasons behind todays gathering, acknowledging the help and co-operation of the Councils and the aim of the Tramway Company to do everything possible to meet the convenience of the public. Having spoken for about ten minutes, he ended his speech by saying:-
*"It is satisfactory to me to feel that in the assistance which has been rendered us in the achievement of our desire to give the public the benefit of the most modern means of traction, the Corporation and District Councils have once more done their duty to the public."*

This brought forth the expected appreciative applause, and then Mr. Alderman Pethick rose to acknowledge the toast and make his reply, followed by further eloquent speeches from Mr. Alfred Lovell, Chairman of St. George District Council, and from Mr. W.D.Strange, Chairman of Kingswood District Council. In his response, Mr. Strange said:-
*"that one of the great advantages of the new system was that the inhabitants of Kingswood could take their families into Bristol to a lecture or entertainment and return by car, instead of having to walk to and from St. George in all kinds of weather."*

A further six speakers rose to their feet in succession, whilst the Assembly Room filled with cigar smoke and mutual admiration.

Separate to the distinguished guests luncheon, the Company had arranged other festivities which included a free 'meat dinner' for 1,200 aged and deserving poor inhabitants of Kingswood and St. George. Local committees representing places of worship in the two District Council areas were set up to organise who came, their seating, and their subsequent consumption of no less than one pound of meat each, plus a bread roll, and collectively 900 buns and scones, 280 lbs of cake, 70 lbs of sugar, and 130 gallons of tea. On the assumption that this was far more than they normally ate, then indigestion must have been rife in St. George and Kingswood that evening, and certainly during the entertainment organised by the Rev. Green of the Bethesda Chapel Redfield. All who attended the meal were then given special tickets for free tram rides. The whole event was virtually given the status of being a public holiday, with local factories and schools closing their doors at mid-day. As the afternoon turned into an autumn evening, many of the principal public buildings along the route were illuminated, whilst the darkness brought with it firework displays to light up the sky.

On the following day the twelve tram-cars 86-97, plus a few horse-cars suitably adapted as trailers, set to work as revenue earners with the start of the first public electric traction service in and around the City of Bristol.

Official compulsory and request tram stops were introduced that day, and in no time the electrified route from Old Market to Kingswood became an unqualified success with the citizens of East Bristol taking the trams to their hearts.

During the third week of operation the following running times were being recorded:

## DOWN JOURNEY (STARTING AT THE DEPOT)

*9 a.m. K'wood to St. George 18 mins. Old Market 15 mins total 33 mins*

*2 p.m. K'wood to St. George 19 mins. Old Market 19 mins total 38 mins*

*3 p.m. K'wood to St. George 20 mins. Old market 23 mins total 43 mins*

Presumably more people used the afternoon trams than in the morning, causing the cars to stop more frequently and take longer at each stop. During this period a number of cars started/finished at *The Kings Arms* in Kingswood, and those that did would save four minutes on their overall journey time.

## UP JOURNEY (STARTING OLD MARKET)

*9 a.m.*
*Old Market to St. George 18 mins. Kingswood 20 mins total 38 mins*
*2 p.m.*
*Old Market to St. George 19 mins. Kingswood 19 mins total 38 mins*
*3 p.m.*
*Old Market to St. George 19 mins. Kingswood 20 mins total 39 mins.*

# THE NEXT FEW YEARS

The Kingswood system continued to be both popular and successful, with no less than 30,000 people being carried by the twelve cars on the first Bank Holiday of 1896. Further details of passengers carried on the Kingswood line were recorded by Mr. Challenger as follows:-

Return of passengers week ended 25 September 1896:

|  | Number Carried | Fare Income £ s d | | |
|---|---|---|---|---|
| Saturday | 19,235 | 121 | 18 | 0 |
| Sunday | 10,268 | 65 | 8 | 5 |
| Monday | 11,143 | 65 | 14 | 6 |
| Tuesday | 9,145 | 53 | 6 | 5 |
| Wednesday | 9,564 | 57 | 2 | 1 |
| Thursday | 9,458 | 56 | 13 | 4 |
| Friday | 8,774 | 50 | 5 | 8 |
|  | 77,587 | 470 | 18 | 5 |

All of the above was achieved by using 9 electric cars, and 6 trailers, thus each vehicle carried on average 740 passengers per day, with each passenger paying a fare of just one-half old penny per journey.

During the month of October 1896, the number of passengers carried fell slightly to the following figures:-

| Week ended | 9 October | 76,506 |
|---|---|---|
| Week ended | 16 October | 74,086 |
| Week ended | 23 October | 72,667 |
| Week ended | 30 October | 68,895 |

Despite this fall in the number of passengers carried, the overall success of the electric tram car encouraged the Company to put in hand plans for the extension of the system, and the conversion of the remaining horse drawn trams to electric traction.

In November 1896 the Capital of the Company was increased to £1,000,000, but all did not go smoothly when a major disagreement occurred with the Corporation of Bristol over who should supply the electric power. The Tramway Company considered that they should be allowed to continue supplying their own electricity not only to the existing system but also to the new routes under consideration. The Corporation disagreed, and refused to allow the Company to carry out the building of further power stations or the extension of existing stations. In retaliation, the Company withdrew its plans for the entire expansion of the existing system. It took over a year before a compromise could be achieved, and eventually in 1898 an Act of Parliament was obtained allowing the Company to proceed with its proposed extensions.

Whilst this argument was in progress, the line from Trinity Church through to Eastville (terminating by Barton Regis Workhouse) was being electrified, with this branch officially opened on 1st February 1897.

Four months later, the Bristol Tramway and Carriage Company Ltd., published 50,000 copies of 'Pictorial Bristol and Handbook' which showed places of interest, a description of each route plus other items of useful information. Reference to the reproductions shown in this book will verify that on the Eastville routes trams started at 5.50 a.m. and ran every few minutes through to 11.30 p.m. on the outward journey from Old Market, with an anticipated travelling time of 12 minutes, (a little faster than in today's traffic) all for the price of one old penny (less than half of 1p).

On the Kingswood route, trams started from Old Market at 5.15 a.m., and continued every few minutes through to 10.49 p.m. The anticipated travelling time was 32 minutes, (somewhat faster than the time recorded by Mr. Challenger in the early days of operating the system, and no doubt brought about by the withdrawal of the horse trams as trailers), and the through fare was 3d or $1^{1}/2$p. With a longer journey, the company set out fare divisions, the first being at Lawrence Hill (GWR station bridge), a penny from Old Market. The second took the passenger as far as Whiteway Road, St. George for twopence, thereafter the charge was three-pence. The company also took this opportunity of reminding passengers that the trams would not stop to take them up or set them down other than at recognised stopping places indicated by white rings painted around the trolley post. Cars running through to Kingswood would be identified by the letter 'K' situated over the canopy, or a lemon yellow light at night, whilst those only running to Whiteway Road would bear the letter 'W' or carry an orange yellow light.

From all routes into Old Market, passengers wishing to go on to the joint railway station at Temple Meads, could board a horse car which ran every 10 minutes from 8.00 a.m. to 11.00 p.m between the Old Market terminus to Totterdown, passing the bottom of the incline some 8 minutes after leaving Old Market.

As 1897 marched towards 1898, the converting of horse drawn lines to electric traction continued so that by the 28 September electric tram cars could reach the *Full Moon* at Fishponds, and just under 10 weeks later they were at their planned terminus at Staple Hill, and housed in the new red-bricked tram depot built at a cost of £6,000.

To cope with this extra electric route mileage, a further 15 cars (Nos.116-118 and 125-136) were purchased and were soon put to work, with the second batch (125-136) of a special low-height construction, and 28ft 3ins long i.e. an extra 4 foot in length being confined to the Fishponds/Staple Hill route to enable them to get under the railway bridge in Fishponds Road near the junction with Muller Road. There is some dispute over the exact details of the low height construction, as according to Charles Challenger's (BTCC's Traffic Manager) tram-

way notebook dated May 1896, the actual height of the tram body remained constant. What was reduced, was the trolley base from 7ft 1in, to 6ft. However, for some reason the top of the platform panel in front of the Driver, remained parallel with the bottom, on the low-height trams, whereas on the standard height vehicles, the top right-hand corner of that panel curved down, indicating that without this feature the panel would foul part of the driving mechanism. In his note-book, Mr. Challenger has drawn the end view of two trams showing common height dimensions of the body and underneath records, "trolley base reduced with a view to pass under Stapleton Road Bridge which is 16ft 2ins centre. Later in the 1920's, the surface of the road level under the bridge was lowered, allowing standard height trams to pass through, and this enabled the Company to rebuild the low-height trams to standard height at their Brislington Works.

The trams were not numbered consecutively, as it was decided to fill the gaps which existed following the withdrawal of the original horse drawn cars.

The pace of work during the following year 1898, slowed down quite considerably following the disagreement with the Corporation of Bristol over the supply of electricity. All of the routes east of Old Market were now electrified and extended to their chosen point of terminus at an average cost of around £7,000 per single track mile (probably around £1,750 million in todays figures). A further 25 trams had arrived, 137-140 being the balance of 4 low-height vehicles built by George F. Milnes & Co. Ltd., 141 an exclusive Directors' car built by the American Car Company, and fitted out quite luxuriously with individual upholstered seats and carpet in the lower saloon. All of the metal work on this particular vehicle was plated, whilst the car had five curtained windows on each side rather than the usual 4 or 3 as in the first batch. It also had a special pale blue and cream livery, and was ornately lined out and panelled. Trams 142-161 were also built in America, but these had a standard revenue earning low-height body.

With a running fleet of 51 cars (not counting the Directors' car), and eight miles of route track, the Company felt that they were now able to abandon the use of trailers, and this feature was finally discontinued on the 15 January 1899.

Although no new construction took place east of Old Market during 1898, several horse lines continued to be built, but using the heavier grade track, these being Old Market to Victoria Street via Tower Hill, St. Philips Bridge and Bath Street, and from the Tramway Centre and Bath Bridge to Arnos Vale, where the Company were constructing their new main works and depot on a five acre site.

Whilst these activities were taking place, work was proceeding behind the scenes to enable new lines to be built once the dispute with the Bristol Corporation was settled. For quite some while the residents of Hanham and nearby St. George had felt that they were 'poor-relations' with regard to public transport, being somewhat isolated by the twin steepness of Air Balloon and Nag's Head Hill, plus Bryant's Hill. Earlier frustrations had been tempered by the fact that they realised the enormous difficulties presented to the equestrian engine in controlling a potential run-away down the hill, only then to have to exert so much effort to drag the vehicle up the other side, but now the Tramway Company had electric traction which could surely ride these hills with grace and so little effort. With Kingswood now connected to the tramway system, why not Hanham, was a view frequently expressed by the Hanham residents during that time.

With the substantial growth in the construction of tramways throughout the country, and the development of electric traction, Acts of Parliament were constantly being promoted to regulate/control the growth of the tramways, as well as to allow new systems to be built. One of the Acts which had a significant bearing on the proposal to extend the line to Hanham was the Light Railways Act 1896. In their wisdom, Members of Parliament had decided that when a tramway system was extended beyond an urban boundary, it ceased to be a tramway and instead became a light railway, under the control of the Act of 1896. As such any plans to extend a light railway were subject to an Official Enquiry to be heard by the Light Railway Commissioners. This the company did in October 1897, and exactly one year later an Order had been presented to both Houses of Parliament by the Commissioners authorising the construction of a light railway to be built from Summerhill Road to Hanham.

## THE ST. GEORGE AND HANHAM LIGHT RAILWAY

During the month of May 1897, an application was made by the Bristol Tramways and Carriage Company Ltd., in pursuance of the Light Railway Act 1896 for an Order to authorise the construction of a light railway from Summerhill Road in the City and County of Bristol to Hanham in the Parish of Kingswood in the County of Gloucestershire. There then followed a special meeting on the 7th July 1897 at which a draft order was submitted, and an Enquiry Hearing held at the Grand Hotel Bristol on the 30th October 1897.

After due consideration and the hearing of any objections, the Commissioners sanctioned the application, and on the 28 November 1898 under the seal of the Board of Trade they published their authorisation for the construction of:-
*"A standard gauge railway 1 mile 4 furlongs 9 chains or*

*thereabouts in length commencing in Summerhill Road (otherwise known as Bath Road) in that part of the Parish of Bristol in the City formerly known as the Parish of St. George in the County of Gloucester by a junction with the termination of the Company's existing tramway in that road passing thence in an easterly direction along that road Air Balloon Hill, Nag's Head Hill, Nag's Head Road, Bryant's Hill and Hanham Street and terminating in the last named street in the village of Hanham in the parish of Kingswood in the County of Gloucestershire at a point 5.15 chains or thereabouts south eastwards from a point in Hanham Street aforesaid opposite or nearly opposite the entrance to Hanham Post Office."*

Work on the new line started as soon as it was financially practicable during the early part of 1899, continuing well into the first year of the new century. With the Board of Trade Inspectors in great demand throughout the country it was not until the 22 December 1900 that the company were given clearance to commence fare paying services between St. George and Hanham. The new-fangled electric tramways had by the birth of the new twentieth century become somewhat 'old hat' and rather common place, and thus the opening of the branch to Hanham had none of the 'razzamatazz' of the Kingswood opening. In quite a short while it seemed perfectly natural and quite ordinary to catch a tram at Hanham and ride the hills to the city boundary and on down to Old Market, the original termination point.

## INTO THE TWENTIETH CENTURY

By now the company had purchased the Finzell's Sugar Warehouse, which was extensively converted to become their new and most up-to-date powerhouse, to meet the extra demands for electricity placed upon them by the ever increasing tramway system. Conveniently situated on the banks of the river next to St. Philips Bridge, the building had originally been built as a chapel. Now empty it was ideally placed for the great quantities of coal to be brought up the river by barge, and was reasonably central to the many tramway routes which radiated out into the suburbs of an expanding city, and beyond. Fortunately this building, unlike the adjoining bridge, escaped the wrath of the German bombers and still stands at Counterslip in all its glory today.

More and more lines were brought into commission as throughout 1899 and 1900 gangs of men and teams of horses toiled and sweated over Redcliffe Hill and on out to Ashton and Bedminster Down, up the steady climb of Gloucester Road to Horfield, as well as filling in gaps around Stokes Croft, City Road and Zetland Road. Probably one of the most difficult new stretches of line to be built at this time was the one which branched off at the Three Lamps, up over the steeply-inclined hill of

Wells Road, past *The Bush* at Totterdown and on up to the *Red Line* at Knowle. Most of this work had been finished by the autumn of 1900, and all that was required, was to have the track and equipment approved by the Board of Trade Inspectors. In early December the new powerhouse at Counterslip was inspected, as was a new spur (siding) which had been installed in Baldwin Street, beside St. Nicholas Church, to act as a terminal point for Knowle (Wells Road) line. All was found to be in order and the lines and powerhouse were 'switched-on'. Just over two weeks later, the other new sections of track were inspected and passed for use, thus with the last Christmas of the old century about to be celebrated, the lights went on along the tracks from Hotwells to Brislington, Zetland Road to the Downs, Gloucester Road to Horfield Barracks, St. George to Hanham, and Totterdown to Knowle.

In anticipation of these new lines coming into use, the Tramway Company ordered no less than 180 standard height identical tram cars from the Midland Railway Carriage & Wagon Company Ltd., of Birmingham, to be built at either their Shrewsbury or Bristol factories. With most of all the old horse cars now taken out of service and scrapped, the Tramway Company were able to use fleet numbers previously held by those cars for the new electric cars now arriving. Accordingly, the first batch of cars to arrive were given the number 1-85, followed by 98-115, then 119-124. During the latter part of 1900 and on into 1901 the remaining 71 trams were delivered and given the fleet numbers 162-232. There were therefore by the end of 1901, no less than 232 open top and open platformed tram cars plying the streets of Bristol and neighbouring districts. With the single exception of the Directors car 141, all of the revenue earning cars were painted blue and white, with the blue panels lined out in ³/4" gold and ¹/8" white. The window frames were ivory colour, ticket boxes and corner posts were scarlet, whilst the stair risers were a dull orange. The saloon was approached through a double bulkhead sliding door, and contained two longitudinal cushioned benches with perforated plywood backs up to window height, each capable of seating twelve persons. The ceiling and the clerestory panel above the ventilator traps, consisted in the main of highly polished birds-eye maple wood, and contained an overhead hand rail and leather strap, plus four unshaded light bulbs, two near the middle, and one at either end. The Tramway Company were very keen to keep the lower saloon free of smoke and both bulkheads displayed a "Smoking Prohibited" sign. They were also keen to provide their passengers with as much reading material as possible, and to this extent the bulkhead doors and side windows contained a wealth of information regarding times of trams, fares, bye-laws and regulations particularly with reference to the rules of the "Kingswood and Hanham Light Railway".

Stairs led from both platforms to the top deck, which being completely open to the elements was much more austere in appearance. All of the seats consisted of a wood slat type, which were transversely fixed to the flooring, with tip-over backs to suit the direction of travel. The only exception to this arrangement were the seats at either end which were permanently fixed to face inwards, and both had room to seat three people. Of the remainder there were eleven doubles and one single (beside the trolley post), providing a total seating for twenty-nine passengers. Peculiar to Bristol Trams at this time was the fitting of Mr. Charles Challenger's patent hinged wooden covers for use in wet weather. This meant that when needing to sit outside on a wet day, it was possible to hinge back covers from the seat to the backrest, thus revealing the dry side of the seat.

Most of the trams were right from the start fitted with enamel advertising signs along both sides of the top deck, plus signs which curved around from the side, to the area above the bulkhead. Whilst many of the signs were more or less permanent, some were made of paper which were stuck to the decency boards.

The next few years were basically used by the Tramway Company to consolidate the enormous changes and expansion which had taken place over the previous three or four years. Apart from a short connection constructed in Barrs Street during 1901, no further new track was laid until 1907 when the Horfield route was extended to Filton.

Nevertheless the company continued to draw-up ambitious plans for the expansion of the system, and in 1904 they had obtained a further Act of Parliament which authorised amongst others the extension of the Kingswood line down the hill to Warmley railway station, and the Hanham route out to the junction of Shellards Road with Bath Road, Longwell Green. Authority was also given to extend the line from Brislington village to Keynsham, with the possibility of persuading the Bath Tramway Company to continue their line from *The Globe* at Newton St. Loe up through Saltford and a linking of the two systems.

Regrettably, none of these ideas ever reached further than the planning stage, the last section to be expanded being across the Downs to Westbury-on-Trym during 1908, Bristol's tramway system was therefore complete with a total route mileage of just under 32 miles.

## THE GOLDEN YEARS
### 1910-1930

With the system established, the ambitious expansion plans shelved, and the early teething problems resolved, the trams settled into a working practise of conveying the citizens of Bristol around in the performance of their working and private lives. Automatic trolley reversers were introduced at certain terminals to make it much easier for the crew to "turn the tram around". Destination details were improved so that by November 1913 service numbers were introduced, together with three lines of route information. The Tramway Centre-Old Market-Kingswood route became number 13, whilst 15 was ascribed to the Hanham-Old Market-Knowle (Bushy Park) route.

The public had really taken the trams and the tramway system to their hearts, and used the conveniently run services as frequently as possible. In fact during the early years of the second decade it would appear as though every man, woman and child took between 2-2$\frac{1}{2}$ tram journeys each week, so that by the end of 1913 it was recorded that Bristol Tramways had in their trams, carried no less than 56,750,000 passengers, i.e. more than the whole population of the United Kingdom.

The next four years were of course mostly affected by the First World War, and its insatiable appetite for men and machines. With Sir George White having completed his plans to build those new-fangled flying machines in and around the little village of Filton, it was just as well that the Horfield line had been extended when it was. In addition, Sir George arranged to have his main tram works at Brislington changed over to the production of aircraft components. With more and more workers being drafted into factories dedicated to help the war effort, more and more journeys were to such an extent that, although 1914 was not a full war year, an additional one and a half million passengers were carried over the figure declared for 1913.

Whilst these extra demands were being placed on the tramway service, the Company had also to suffer the effects of the country calling men to arms. By the end of 1915 a quarter of the male employees had enlisted, and the Company was left with no other alternative but to turn to the difficult decision of employing women as conductresses. At a time when it was still a prevalent male conception that women were not capable of carrying out 'mens work', and in any case their place was in the home, such a decision took a great deal of courage, both on the part of the potential employer, and also on the part of those spirited and radical minded women who applied to fill the vacancies. Although the employment of women was given official approval in November 1916, it was not until 1 January 1917 that the first women took out a tram as a conductress. Those that joined the Tramway Company were immaculately kitted out in a long uniform skirt and jacket, with polished buttons and shiny boots. Quickly accepted by the travelling public, they soon became affectionately known as "clippies". Only young women of between 18-25 years of age were accepted, and they were required to work a 54-hour week, for which they were paid 23 shillings. (£1.15). Despite the long hours and small reward, many of the women discovered for the very first time a certain amount of financial freedom which, they were reluctant to give up when the war ended. Of those men who could and did came back to reclaim their job, a number found that it was still occupied by these "new young clippies", which meant that he was either offered menial low-paid work around the depot, or he was out on the dole. Such a situation inevitably led to a great deal of unrest, and it was not unknown for trams to be stopped by gangs of unemployed men, who then proceeded to turn off all of the passengers and crew before breaking the tram windows and carrying out other damage. By the time no less than 30 trams had been subjected to such damage, and with public sympathy firmly on the side of the men, the Company eventually decided to get rid of the remaining conductresses with the inducement of a "golden hand-shake" of £5 each.

After the war years it was necessary for the Company to pick-up the pieces, and to review its future in the light of developments which had taken place during the past four years. In particular a lot of work had been carried out on the internal-combustion engine to improve its reliability, and to widen its use, as well as the expansion of Mr. Dunlop's development of pneumatic tyres. Thus in the years immediately following the war, there was a substantial expansion of the motor-bus as an important means of public transport. Not being confined to the limitations imposed by tram tracks, buses were more comfortable and more mobile than trams, and soon began to compete directly with the tramway system.

However, this is not to say that the Company, who also ran the buses, neglected its trams or its tramway network. With the gradual return of a male workforce, and the increased availability of materials, work began on a programme of improvements, mostly in connection with the running track which was re-laid, and where possible single track was doubled.

Around this time one of the bridges over the railway line at Lawrence Hill was widened, and this meant that for a time not only was the line to Old Market swivelled across towards the pavement, arrangements had to be introduced so that outward bound cars could use the same section of track, and then vice versa when the other side of the road was being worked upon. However despite the extra work involved, the disruption to this frequently used route was kept to an absolute minimum.

It was not only the track, poles and overhead wires that received attention, as during the 1920's work was put in hand at the Company's Brislington Works for a thorough overhaul/refurbishment of the tram fleet. Prior to this an order for six new trams was given to the works, and during 1920 cars 233-237 appeared, each of them built to the identical design of the original standard cards built twenty-five years previously. The theoretical oldest car in the fleet was number 86, and with the need to develop a rail-grinding vehicle, it was decided to take number 86 out of service for this purpose, and for some reason to reissue that number to one of the six new cars now coming into service. With the road under the railway bridge at Eastville now lowered, there was no longer the need to have the original short wheeled low deck trams, and these were gradually rebuilt with the longer standard height bodies. Each conversion took a team of three men six weeks to complete, thus as the 1920's developed Bristol had, at 237, the largest fleet of standardised open-top trams in the country, with apparently no desire to modernise it, or improve the quality of travel for an itinerant public who were becoming more and more sophisticated and demanding in the comfort of their travel. Whilst other towns and cities were improving their Victorian trams with covered top decks, better trams with more comfortable seating, and even protection for the crews, particularly for the driver, Bristol as so often happens stuck with what they had, and the spirit of adventure which had driven the promoters of the tramway system to achieve so much floundered on the concern that if improved, someone else might have made money out of them. Strangely when car 86 was converted into a rail-grinder, it not only had its platform shortened, it had a canopy built over the platform providing the driver with some, if fairly minimal, protection from the rain, which was much more than any of the service trams received.

The fleet of 237 cars was reduced to 234 in 1923, when it was decided (for reasons not known) to withdraw trams 92, 116 and 117 from active service.

During the mid-1920's it was decided to dispense with the route numbers introduced ten years previously, and to replace the use of destination slides with the new roller blinds. These carried a series of destinations made up from bold stencilled letters which were placed on the material. The material was then sprayed black and the letters removed so that when fitted in the display box, the light at the back would shine through and illuminate the displayed destination at night. The removal of the numbers coincided with some of the routes being altered, so that the Hanham-Knowle run was extended from Bushy Park to the *Red Lion* in Wells Road, whilst the short working, Old Market-St. George, was replaced by increased workings to either Whiteway Road, (later to be more frequently shown as Marling Road on the destination blinds) or Nags Head Hill (Top). In both instances the tram would, upon reaching its destination, reverse back down the up track for a short while and cross over on the points to the down track, whilst the conductor manually reversed the trolley. This meant that the timing of when the tram reached its destination was critical if it was to avoid impeding either the outward or inward long haul tram. In the rest of the network, routes were either amalgamated or left unchanged with only the Ashton Gate terminus slightly shortened, and the Temple Meads siding closed. This was the last change made to the network prior to when routes were finally abandoned.

Despite having flirted with, and constructed two prototype trolleybuses, Bristol clung on to their beloved trams even though the early years of the third decade had seen further and continued improvements in buses as well as a greater number being introduced to clog up the city streets. By 1933 totally enclosed double-decker buses were conveying the citizens of Bristol around in every increasing comfort, and the writing was beginning to appear on the wall that the days of the tramcars were numbered.

Changes were at this time being made to the livery of the tram, with the gradual abandonment of the Victorian ornate, to a more pragmatic and simplified style. As each tram passed through the paintshop the title BRISTOL TRAMWAYS & CARRIAGE CO. LTD. along the rocker panel was removed, the style of the shaded fleet number on the dash panel was changed to a more simplified design. The panel lining was less ornate, with the gold leaf being replaced by yellow paint, whilst the wrought iron grille by the stairs was covered with a paper advertising panel.

With all of the trams now built/re-built to a standard pattern and size, their depot allocation was only affected by the trolley and reverser position. Because of their construction and use, a trolley could not be turned through a complete circle. If it had been allowed to do so then the connecting internal electrical wires would soon have become twisted and dangerous, with no easy way of "undoing" the spiral. The trolley arm was therefore blocked so that it was restricted to move within a maximum arc of 270 degrees, with the bulk of the movement taking place over the outside of the tram, (the trolley posts were off-centre both by length and breadth). The Ward's patented trolley reverser was basically a triangle of wires at the terminus, so that having arrived at its destination, and discharged its passengers, the driver walked through the tram with the single driving handle, and after fitting it onto the square end of the controller would slowly drive the tram forward whilst is boom (inclined upward under pressure of 25lbs) kept the swivel head still in its original trailing position. With the trolley head now being "pushed", it was soon automatically taken away from the running wire by means of a set point, and run through to the apex of the triangle, then the continued forward movement of the tram caused the trolley head to run down the second part of the triangle before it returned to the running line, and was once again in a trailing position.

The reversing triangle was either set to the left or to the right of the running track, according to the amount of space available, and thus it was necessary for the traffic manager, (and of course the driver) to ensure that a left handed tram was matched with a left handed reverser or a right handed tram/reverser combination according to the layout at the terminus, otherwise the reverser would not work and damage could be done to the trolley. Thus there was a great advantage to ensure that certain trams were kept to particular routes, which in turn meant that those certain trams were always allocated to a specific depot. The Kingswood depot was situated at the terminus in the High Street, and could house just 19 trams, and thus cars 170-188 were stabled there during most of the 1930's, these being kept solely on the Kingswood-Tramway Centre service. Similarly the Beaconsfield Road depot at St. George could also hold 19 trams, and its allocation during this time were cars 160-169, 192-195, 197-201, all kept on the Hanham-Knowle route.

Throughout the whole lifetime of the trams they carried a range of advertisements, the most notable being made up of vitreous enamel sheets along the decency boards, plus a curved plate at each end of the tram linking the board with the top of the stairs plus, from the mid 20's, a board covering the wrought-iron grill under the stairs. In addition many less permanent advertisements and notices were pasted to the inside of the windows. As fashions changed so did the advertisements, but during the 1930's and on to the closure of the network the most frequent signs to be seen on the decency boards were for "Ovaltine", "Kelloggs", "Shop at Jones", and "Henry Jones Flour". Perhaps the most famous or most remembered was the advertisement for "Harris" purveyors of bacon, sausages and meat pies. By 1932 they had obtained the exclusive use of one end of every tram in the fleet, with their wrap around vitreous enamel advertisement, and on trams 1-12, plus 86 they had the full monopoly of both ends. Other signs advertised "Georges Beers", "Dunlop Tyres", and one which still exists today "Wear an Andersons and ride on top".

Despite the continued public interest and liking for their unique and reliable trams, this was the start of the twilight years for the tramway system. The Corporation of Bristol laid out plans in 1936 for a new City Centre to cover part of St. Augustines Reach with a large flower bed, and a wide road from Colston Avenue through to College Green, plus a new inner road from Broad Quay through Redcliffe to Old Market, and such plans did not provide for the old trams. Other changes were being mooted, including the introduction of more and more modern buses, with their greater flexibility.

The future of the tramway system was discussed throughout 1937, with the Company signing an agreement with the Transport and General Workers Union to provide security for the 1,000 or so employees directly involved with the running of the trams, in the event of the service being abandoned. Other discussions took place and the City was rife with rumours as to the fate of the tramway. In January 1938, a local newspaper announced that 200 buses, all of them made in Bristol would soon be seen on the city streets as replacements for the trams. By the end of April notice was given by the Western Area Traffic Commissioners that in early May the Westbury-Centre, Hotwells-Centre, and Eastville-Durdham Downs tram routes would close and be replaced by buses. Thus on Saturday, 7 May 1938, car 46 made the last journey from Westbury to the Centre, whilst other trams made similar journeys from Hotwells and Durdham Downs. Somewhat ignominiously, car 46 was followed by a tower wagon and crew who proceeded

to dismantle the overhead wires, thus preventing any second thoughts of keeping the line open. Throughout the following day there was a procession of no less than thirty-four trams which made their way to Kingswood, and into the depot where at the back, a hole had been made in the wall through which the track and overhead wires had been laid out in two large looping sidings built especially to accommodate the trams designated to be scrapped.

The sidings were laid out on sleepers and followed the boundary wall alongside Holly Mill Road and Alma Road. The first car through was 208 of the Brislington-Hotwells route, and this was very quickly followed by the other thirty-three cars so that by the evening of the 8 May 1938, the siding was almost full. The following day workmen began stripping 208 of its top deck fittings, and when this was done the body of the tram was pulled over, off the trucks, and set on fire. The trucks went for scrap, (mostly to Habgood's and Pugsley's) the wooden seats sold quite well to the general public, mostly as garden seats, and from time to time souvenir hunters found something to their liking. It was unfortunately the beginning of the end, and by the 24 June 1938 all trace of those thirty-four beloved trams had disappeared for ever, having had a scrap value of no more than £25.

## DOWN BUT NOT OUT, THE FINAL YEARS OF PEACE.

With almost a touch of indecent haste, the next lines scheduled for 'the axe' were Bristol Bridge-Bedminster Down, and Bristol Bridge-Ashton Gate, due to be closed on the 22 July 1938, but this was delayed and instead the next route to be closed was part of the Hanham-Knowle line, being that section from Old Market-Knowle. Thus on the 3 September 1938 the last tram left the *Red Lion* terminus complete with a barrel of beer which was gradually consumed as farewell drinks were passed around whilst the car made its way to Old Market. Elsewhere in the city other routes were also being closed down including Staple Hill-Old Market, and Brislington-Tramway Centre, and in a number of incidents the public more vociferous as they celebrated/mourned the passing of the trams. Souvenir hunters were out in force as were those just bent on mayhem, with car 101 limping back into the Brislington Depot shorn of seats, cushions, advertising panels, hand-rails and anything else that could be removed. At Staple Hill car 129 performed a closing ceremony by being 'pulled' across the City/Gloucestershire boundary by two horses as it made its final trip to the terminus at the junction of Broad Street with Teewell Hill. On its return journey the driver, Arthur Brittan, recalled how there were many fireworks being let off, and the passengers were all becoming more boisterous. However, two of the passengers on this overcrowded tram were a little more industrious with their time, as one decided to relieve the car of its curtains, so that they could be re-fitted in his greenhouse, whilst the other spent all of the time cutting the chain around the platform, considering that it would make a fine leash. Nevertheless, car 129 was able to reach its final resting place at Kingswood under its 'own steam', which is more than can be said for ten other trams which were so badly damaged, by the revellers that night, that they each needed to be towed in by rescue parties specially sent out by the Kingswood Depot Manager. In total a further thirty trams went that night to the graveyard, with many still carrying passengers who insisted on staying on the cars whilst they were driven through the hole and out on to the siding. Even then it took the strong arm of the law to eventually persuade the well-wishers that it was time to go home.

By the end of October a further fifty-six trams had been totally scrapped at Kingswood, including car 237 one of the last batch of trams built for the company, and then only nineteen years old, compared with most of the others being scrapped which were forty-nine to fifty-four years old. Its sister trams 233 and 234 followed with nineteen other cars torched by the end of the year. Thus as 1939 dawned, the tram fleet had literally been cut back by almost half with one hundred and eleven trams now but just a memory.

Problems still existed over the intended closure of the westward routes out through Bedminster, but this did not prevent the Corporation from going ahead with its plans to rid the Tramway Centre of its namesake. Thus it was now the time for the Kingswood route to be pruned, and on the 15 July 1939, the city terminus was brought back from the centre to Old Market, with car 231 taking the honours of being the last fare carrying tram to operate out of the Centre.

With other closures taking place that night a further fifty-six cars were withdrawn from service, with most of them being driven straight through to the Kingswood graveyard, leaving just sixty-six trams in the capital fleet.

As the hot summer of 1939 developed, the talk of war with Germany increased, and the prospects of food and fuel shortages, as well as the fear of hordes of Nazi planes bombing the city, occupied the minds of most people. The Tramway Company in conjunction with Bristol. Corporation still had 'October pencilled in' as the month when the trams of Bristol would be totally abandoned, but the outbreak of war on the 3 September 1939 meant that the closure plans needed to be put 'on the back burner'. After all more buses meant more petrol to be consumed, and petrol was not only in short supply, it also had to run the gauntlet of the U-boat menace, thus as much as possible had to be saved, and the trams would be reprieved.

## WAR WORK

The abandonment of the network had taken its toll, with all the routes closed with the exception of just two with four destinations, i.e. Bristol Bridge out to the *London Inn* Bedminster, where the track divided with one route going through to Ashton Gate, and the other passing Bedminster Depot on its way to the other end of Winterstoke Road, stopping almost on the railway bridge of the Great Western's main line to the West Country. Unconnected by any service route, but still physically connected by track to its twin, the other line ran from Old Market out through St. George to the fountain where it divided, with one route going up the hill to Kingswood, whilst the other negotiated the 'switch-back' hills to Hanham. To operate these routes, the company had in its capital fleet just sixty-three ageing trams, plus half (86, 235 and 236) of the batch of six, which had been built at Brislington in 1920 and were thus less than twenty years old. In reserve the company, in anticipation of the war, had halted the scrapping of six cars from the fifty-six withdrawn from service in July 1939. Thus at the outbreak of the war, cars 13/24/47/138/144 and 210 remained on the Kingswood siding, as a strategic reserve, whilst twenty-four active cars squeezed into and out of the Kingswood Depot, leaving a further twenty three cars at Bedminster, and nineteen cars at Beaconsfield Road.

The war brought with it the immediate fear of enemy bombing, and in particular the concern that we must not encourage the German Bombers on their nightly raids by showing lights to guide them to their target. Much thought had been given by the Civil Defence Authorities about this problem, which could only be solved by a complete 'black-out'. Street lighting was turned off, homes and factories had to fix black material over the windows so that no light was shown at night, traffic had to drive around on one very dim light, and more civilians were killed on the roads, than died as a result of enemy action!! The trams were not exempt from the black-out, and one of the first effects was for the fenders, truck sides, platform steps and sandboxes to be painted white. In addition, all of the lights were screened, and window tops painted black, including the destination boxes. The only black-out precaution the Tramway Company could not take was against the electrical flashes as the trolley head passed over a connector, and this gave rise to a number of people expressing concern and worry that the trams would act as a magnet to the German Bombers.

The initial fears of bombing raids over Bristol did not materialise as the phoney war developed and its was left to the soldiers, sailors and airmen to face the hazards of the war. Bristol remained unscathed, and even became a "safe area" where school children from London could be evacuated. Those responsible for public transport saw less and less reason not to continue with their plans to 'be rid of those confounded tram cars', and even announced on the 2 May 1940 that the trams are to finish as the replacement buses become available and adequate supplies of fuel were released. This however was not to happen, particularly with so much of our crude oil being sent to the bottom of the sea.

Within the Tramway Company plans were made to keep the trams going for the duration and these included putting car 158 through the paint shop, to emerge in an austere livery of unlined blue and white. Around the same time one or two other trams had their trucks changed so that those particular cars could be kept going.

With the fall of France bringing Bristol much close to the range of German Bombers, air-raid warnings became more frequent, and on the 25 June 1940 the first bombs fell around the Brislington and Temple Meads area. Whilst the early raids were of a relatively minor nature, trams and buses were halted during the period of the alert, although this was subsequently relaxed so that the public transport only stopped when it was reported that the enemy planes were overhead. Apart from the bombs themselves, there was always the danger from shrapnel which was created not only when the bombs exploded, but also when the anti-aircraft shells exploded, and thus sections of the highway/tram track could at any time have small or large pieces of shrapnel spread over quite a wide area. Buses may have had the opportunity of driving around the shrapnel or other items of debris, but this was a luxury not afforded the trams, and as a consequence it was necessary for the Company to make special arrangements to have the track cleared of any obstructions. In the past they would have used one of the two specially adapted vehicles in the fleet fixed with a large cylindrical brush, which was used to clear the track, mostly of snow. By now these vehicles had passed through the yard at Kingswood and no longer existed, and thus it was necessary to keep a "track-cleaning car" at each depot, with the sole purpose of going out over the route before the service trams restarted their work, with a gang of men on board and a keen eyed driver to keep a lookout for such obstructions. 125 was the car earmarked for this work at the Bedminster Depot, whilst 126 and 199 performed these duties at Kingswood and St. George respectively.

The first major blitz of the war to hit Bristol occurred on the evening of the 24 November 1940. Redcliffe Street suffered quite badly on that night, making it impossible for traffic to get through, which meant that trams running in from Bedminster Down and Ashton Gate had to terminate their journeys on Redcliffe Hill. In the meanwhile the overhead wires along Clarence Road, Redfield were down, preventing the Hanham and Kingswood trams getting into Old Market. Most of the effort to restore the system was concentrated on Redcliffe Street, and despite further damage which occurred a few nights later, the new track, poles and wiring were in place within a week. Repairing the overhead system

along Clarence Road took a little longer, causing passengers to have to walk half a mile or so to the city terminus.

As 1940 came to an end, the Tramway Company had coped with its first real test of the war in maintaining the much reduced tram service, and despite the difficulties were ready to face the New Year with confidence.

Regrettably that confidence was shattered a few days into the New Year when, at around 6 a.m. on the morning of 4 January 1941, a large bomb hit the portals at the entrance of Bedminster Depot killing the driver of car 71, which was about to leave the depot to start an early morning workman's turn. Car 164 which was also near the entrance was, with No.71, a complete write-off, whilst cars 87, 136 and 236 were seriously damaged by blast. Moments previously, cars 9 and 26 had left the depot to start their days work, with No.9 on its way up West Street to Bedminster Down, but before it had got far it was caught in the blast of another bomb, which was so severe that the tram ended up leaning against a butcher's shop, with the front-end in the bedroom windows. No26 fared better but had had all of its windows shattered by blast. So ended the south Bristol section of the tramway system, leaving Kingswood and Hanham to be the last outpost of what had once been a very fine and well loved public transport network.

The bombing of the Bedminster Depot, and resulting closure of the south Bristol routes gave further ammunition to the anti-tram lobby, and with buses being used to replace the trams on the Ashton Gate and Bedminster Down routes, it was soon being suggested as early as March 1941, that these new bus routes be extended to Hanham and Kingswood respectively.

This however did not happen, and the trams continued to run to Kingswood and Hanham throughout February and March of that year, and even on into April. The anti-tram lobby did however have an unexpected ally in high places who decided that Good Friday, the 11 April 1941 would be as good a day as any to close down Bristol's tramway system once and for all.

As dusk began to settle over Bristol on that first Easter day, the air-raid sirens heralded what was to become one of the longest blitzes of the war over the city. Despite the fear of enemy planes overhead, the public transport system tried to keep to a respectable time-table during the Good Friday evening. Trams to and from Kingswood and Hanham to Old Market made their way to the accompaniment of the drone from enemy aircraft, the thump thump from anti-aircraft batteries, and dull rolling sound like distant thunder, as bombs found their target, and sent up a bright flash as they exploded. On the inward journeys, the driver was faced with a reddish glowing sky, which was occasionally changed by dancing flashes, as the clouds reflected the many fires in the city, started by numerous incendiaries dropped by the Luftwaffe path finders, and the explosion of the bombs as they found their target. There was the fear that by heading towards the centre of town was like driving into a maelstrom of fire and destruction, and thus most of the crews felt happier in taking their charge back to the outskirts and their anticipated safety.

Around 9.45 p.m. on that holocaust evening there remained just two trams left in Old Market, one ready to take the last of the days journeys through to Kingswood, the other to work the truncated Hanham route, terminating at Marling Road, before heading back to the depot at Beaconsfield Road. The first tram to leave had on its heavily shaded destination box the description Marling Road, and with few passengers on board journeying unhindered through Lawrence Hill, and Redfield, and past the fountain at St. George arriving at Marling Road around 10.10 p.m.

The last run to Kingswood was scheduled to leave Old Market at 10.00 p.m. and in those last few minutes leading up to the hour both Driver Webster, and his conductor, Arthur Brittan were anxious to get away from the centre of town. Tomorrow would be another day for the trams, but for tonight, to get off home as safely as possible, was about all that the crew, and the small number of passengers could really think of doing. As the large hand of Mr. Webster's timepiece pointed upwards, he released the brake and set his tram in motion. Soon he was running through Lawrence Hill and Redfield in the wake of the Marling Road tram, on up the continuous climb to St. George, avoiding his predecessor as he returned his charge to Beaconsfield Road, taking the left-hand point at the fountain, and on, climbing up Clouds, Bell and Two Mile Hills. The sounds of war were being gradually left behind, whilst ahead lay the darkness of the country-side, and home. Having gained Regent Street without hindrance or incident, both driver and conductor felt that they could begin to relax, after all the depot was less than a mile away, the enemy bombs were falling three or four miles away, so what could go wrong, it was just a straight run into the depot.

Once on the level of Regent Street, Driver Webster was able to open out the power enabling the car to gather speed as it passed the Clock Tower and entered High Street. If he was able to see the clock Mr. Webster would have noticed that it was just coming up to 10.30 p.m., but whatever he was doing at that moment, his attention was very quickly taken by an apparent momentary loss of power, and the flickering of the dimmed lights, which within seconds turned to a situation of no lights and no power. Very quickly his charge free-wheeled to a halt, and nothing Driver Webster could do would bring life back into the tramcar. By chance the tram was standing on the only section of track, running out from Old Market to Kingswood, that ran down-hill, and not only that, it ran down-hill all the way to the depot. It was by now very obvious that there had been a major

power failure somewhere in the system, and accordingly Arthur Brittan with the help of one or two onlookers and gravity agreed to push the tram home. With Driver Webster at the controls the last revenue earning tram as it was subsequently to become, ended its journey freewheeling through the Kingswood depot and coming to a rest on the tightly-curved fan of rails which made up the scrap yard.

Unknown to anyone at Kingswood at that time was the fact that a bomb had ploughed through "Ha'penny" Bridge St. Philips and severed the power lines which connected Counterslip power station with the remaining tramway system. All of the trams were in their respective depots so there really was nothing more that could be done until the morning, when hopefully the power would be restored.

After the previous nights bombardment, workers still needed to get to work, even if it was Easter Saturday, and many in the Kingswood, Hanham and St. George areas left their homes as usual to walk to the nearest tram stop to await that friendly and reassuring sound of the tramcar coming their way. Jerry had after all been overhead during the night, and no doubt a great deal of damage had been done, but it was back to work as usual, with an air of defiance which said that we are not going to be beaten, we will carry on as normal. There was however something very different about this particular morning for those who waited in anticipation, a stillness in the air which was not disturbed by the distant sound of their friendly tram, instead they were greeted with the sight, sound and smell of unfamiliar buses pulling up alongside the tram stop, with an ingratiating conductor advising them to climb on board as quickly as possible. "Where's the tram then?", or "whot, no tram?" was the frequent question thrown at the over-worked conductor, who rarely knew the correct reason for the trams demise. Left to speculate amongst themselves, the verdict was that with no trams about, Jerry must have hit Bristol very hard last night, and may even have dealt her a mortal blow.

History tells us that this was of course not the case, it had been a major raid, and as it subsequently turned out it was the last major raid to take place in the skies over the City. Whilst Bristol was not mortally wounded, one bomb had achieved what many bureaucrats had been trying to do for years, close the tramway system once and for all. The damage to the St. Philips's bridge was too much to do, the bridge itself would need to be rebuilt, and no bridge meant that the power cables could not be carried across the river. Just over a month after the fatal bomb had fallen the decision was taken to formally announce the abandonment of the tramway.

By early June, all of the trams trapped in their depot at Beaconsfield Road were pulled out and towed to Kingswood, where they joined almost two dozen other trams on "death row" to await their ultimate fate. The work of breaking them up continued at a fairly leisurely pace, throughout the summer months and on into the autumn, with the last passenger tram No.64 succumbing to the breaker's skill on the 16 October 1941. This was followed by the destruction of the Grinder No.1 car, and Plough No.2 car on the twentieth of that month.

Thus ended the illustrious history of the Bristol Trams, who faithfully and safely served the city and surrounding areas for 70 years. In all of that time there had only been three accidents and only one of them resulted in a fatality.

What a different story it might have been had that one bomb gone straight into the river rather than hitting the smaller object of the bridge. With a scrap value of just £25 each when they were broken up, none were preserved, and all that fortunately remains is a collection of photographs, showing the Bristol Tram in all its glory.

---

BRISTOL TRAMWAYS AND CARRIAGE COMPANY, LIMITED. 61

# City, St. George and Kingswood Electric Tramways.

WEEK DAYS.—KINGSWOOD TO ST. GEORGE AND OLD MARKET.

First cars depart at 5.15 a.m., 5.19, 5.25, 6.20, 6.36, 6.55, 7.13, and then every few minutes until 10.49 p.m.

WHITEWAY ROAD TO OLD MARKET.

First cars depart at 5.28 a.m., 5.32, 5.38, 6.33, 6.49, 7.8, 7.26, and then every few minutes until 11.5 p.m.

LAWRENCE HILL (G.W.R.) TO OLD MARKET.

First cars depart at 5.33 a.m., 5.38, 5.43, 5.46, 5.50, 6.44, 7.0, 7.19, 7.37, then every few minutes until 11.19 p.m.

OLD MARKET TO WHITEWAY ROAD OR KINGSWOOD.

First cars depart at 5.45 a.m., 5.55, 6.5, 6.15, 7.1, 7.12, 7.30, 7.48, then every few minutes until 11 p.m. to Kingswood and 11.30 p.m. to Whiteway Road.

LAWRENCE HILL (G.W.R.) TO WHITEWAY ROAD OR KINGSWOOD.

First cars depart at 5.54 a.m., 6.4, 6.14, 6.24, 7.10, 7.21, 7.39, 7.57, and then every few minutes until 11.8 p.m. to Kingswood and 11.38 p.m. to Whiteway Road.

WHITEWAY ROAD TO KINGSWOOD.

First cars depart at 4.58 a.m., 5.3, 5.8, 6.5, 6.15, 6.25, 6.35, 7.8, 7.21, 7.32, 7.43, 7.50, 8.8, and then every few minutes until 11.20 p.m.

SUNDAYS.—Cars run every few minutes.

KINGSWOOD to OLD MARKET—First car 2.25 p.m., last 9.49 p.m.
WHITEWAY ROAD to OLD MARKET—First car 2.8 p.m., last 10.2 p.m.
LAWRENCE HILL to OLD MARKET—First car 2.13 p.m., last 10.13 p.m.
OLD MARKET to KINGSWOOD—First car 2.24 p.m., last 10 p.m.; to WHITEWAY ROAD 10.30 p.m.
LAWRENCE HILL to KINGSWOOD—First car 2.33 p.m., last 10.9 p.m.; to WHITEWAY ROAD 10.39 p.m.
WHITEWAY ROAD to KINGSWOOD—First car 2.8 p.m., last 10.20 p.m.

# City, St. George and Kingswood Electric Tramways.—*Continued.*

### FARE DIVISION STATIONS.

The Fare Divisions are at the following Stations, namely :—LAWRENCE HILL (G.W.R.) and WHITEWAY ROAD. All cars stop at these Stations, and passengers entering the cars before they are brought to a standstill, and before those alighting leave the car, will be charged full fare for the section which terminates at such Station.

### STOPPING PLACES.

Cars will not stop to take up or set down passengers except at the Stations and Stopping Places indicated by Rings painted around the trolley posts. At the "Fare Division Stations," as named above, all cars will stop; but at other intermediate Stopping Places, cars will stop only when required for passengers to alight or by intending passengers who wish to be taken up.

### DISTINGUISHING SIGNALS.

*The cars running through to Kingswood are distinguished by letter "K" over the canopy, and by Lemon Yellow Front Light at night.*

*Those cars running only as far as Whiteway Road exhibit a letter "W" over the canopy, and a board across the side windows, lettered "Whiteway Road only," and carry an Orange Yellow Front Light at night.*

### ELECTRIC SIGNAL BELLS.

Electric Signal Bells are provided inside and outside for the use of passengers. When they wish the car stopped passengers should just before reaching a stopping place, ring the bell, and the Conductor will signal the Motorman to stop on arrival there.

*Time occupied on journey.* To or from KINGSWOOD and OLD MARKET, 32 minutes.
To or from WHITEWAY ROAD and OLD MARKET, 20 minutes.
To or from LAWRENCE HILL and OLD MARKET, 9 minutes.

*Time Tables giving fuller details are exhibited on the car windows.*

## FARES:—(either way.)

| | |
|---|---|
| Old Market and Lawrence Hill (G.W.R.) - - - - | 1d. |
| Lawrence Hill (G.W.R.) and Whiteway Road - - - | 1d. |
| Whiteway Road and Kingswood - - - - | 1d. |
| Old Market and Whiteway Road - - - - | 2d. |
| Lawrence Hill (G.W.R.) and Kingswood - - - - | 2d. |
| Old Market and Kingswood (THE ALL WAY) - - - - | 3d. |

# PART 2

# THE JOURNEY

# OUTWARD BOUND

# HANHAM ✽ ✽ KNOWLE

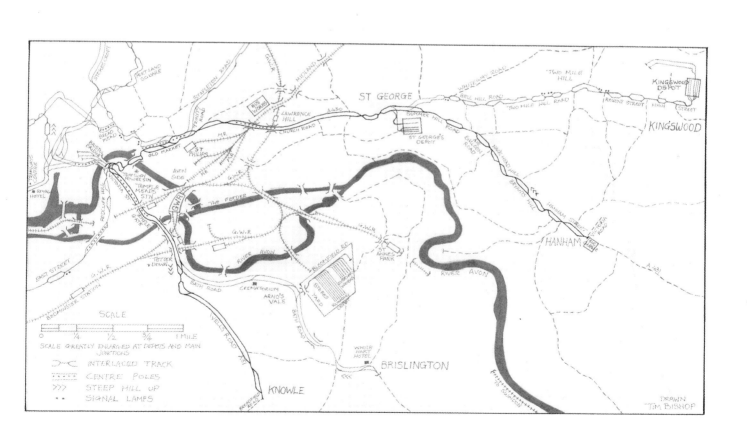

# The Bristol Tramways and Carriage Company, Limited.

## TIME TABLE.

# HANHAM, St. GEORGE, OLD MARKET & BUSHY PARK

## HANHAM TO OLD MARKET AND BUSHY PARK.

**MONDAYS TO FRIDAYS**

| | |
|---|---|
| **HANHAM** for OLD MARKET. | 5.15, 5.21, 5.30, 5.35, 5.50, 6.5, 6.20, 6.27, 6.40, 6.53, 7.2, 7.12, 7.22, 7.30, 7.45, 8.0, 8.15, 8.22, 8.30, 8.45, 9.0, 9.15, 9.27, 9.36 a.m. AFTER 9.36 a.m. EVERY SEVEN MINUTES until 7.45 p.m. AFTER 7.45 p.m. EVERY TEN MINUTES until 11.0 p.m. |
| For BUSHY PARK. | 7.30, 7.45, 8.0, 8.15, 8.22, 8.30, 8.45, 9.0, 9.15, 9.27, 9.36 a.m. AFTER 9.36 a.m. EVERY SEVEN MINUTES until 7.45 p.m. AFTER 7.45 p.m. EVERY TEN MINUTES until 10.35 p.m. |
| **MARLING ROAD** For OLD MARKET. | From ST. GEORGE DEPOT 5.0 a.m. From MARLING ROAD 5.23, 5.29, 5.38, 5.43, 5.58, 6.13, 6.28, 6.35, 6.48, 7.1, 7.10, 7.20, 7.30, 7.38, 7.53, 8.8, 8.23, 8.30, 8.38, 8.53, 9.8, 9.23, 9.36, 9.44 a.m. AFTER 9.44 a.m. EVERY SEVEN MINUTES until 7.53 p.m. AFTER 7.53 p.m. EVERY TEN MINUTES until 11.8 p.m. |
| For BUSHY PARK. | 7.38, 7.53, 8.8, 8.23, 8.30, 8.38, 8.53, 9.8, 9.23, 9.35 a.m. AFTER 9.35 a.m. EVERY SEVEN MINUTES until 7.33 p.m. AFTER 7.33 p.m. EVERY TEN MINUTES until 10.43 p.m. |
| **VICTORIA ROAD** for OLD MARKET. | 5.4, 5.18, 5.28, 5.30, 5.32, 5.33, 5.36, 5.37, 5.41, 5.44, 5.45, 5.45½, 5.47, 5.50, 6.5, 6.14, 6.20, 6.23, 6.24, 6.28, 6.33, 6.35, 6.37, 6.42, 6.43, 6.50, 6.55, 6.58, 7.4, 7.8, 7.13, 7.17, 7.20, 7.22, 7.24, 7.26, 7.28, 7.30, 7.31, 7.34, 7.36, 7.37, 7.38, 7.41, 7.42, 7.44, 7.45, 7.47. |
| For BUSHY PARK. | 7.45, 7.54, 8.0 a.m. then EVERY SEVEN MINUTES until 8.0 p.m. AFTER 8.0 p.m. EVERY TEN MINUTES until 10.50 p.m. |

## BUSHY PARK TO OLD MARKET AND HANHAM.

**MONDAYS TO FRIDAYS.**

| | |
|---|---|
| **BUSHY PARK** for HANHAM. | 8.14, 8.29, 8.43, 8.51 a.m., then EVERY SEVEN MINUTES until 6.52 p.m., then 7.6, 7.21, 7.28, 7.36, 7.51, 7.58, 8.6, 8.15, 8.27 p.m. AFTER 8.27 p.m. EVERY TEN MINUTES until 10.58 p.m. At 10.58, 11.8, 11.19 to MARLING ROAD only. |
| **OLD MARKET** for HANHAM. | 5.25, 5.44, 5.49D, 5.55, 6.0D, 6.2, 6.4D, 6.10, 6.22, 6.27D, 6.36, 6.37D, 6.42D, 6.50, 6.51D, 7.0, 7.8D, 7.10, 7.17D, 7.21D, 7.30, 7.33D, 7.37D, 7.39D, 7.41, 7.43D, 7.47D, 7.49D, 7.51, 7.54D, 8.0, 8.15, 8.28, 8.36D, 8.43, 8.50D, 8.57, 9.5 a.m. AFTER 9.5 a.m. EVERY SEVEN MINUTES until 6.37 p.m., then 6.44, 6.52, 6.59, 7.6, 7.20, 7.35, 7.42, 7.50, 8.5, 8.12, 8.20, 8.29, 8.41 p.m. AFTER 8.41 p.m. EVERY TEN MINUTES until 11.10 p.m. D to St. George Depot only. |
| For MARLING ROAD. (St. George). | 5.25, 5.44, 5.55, 6.2, 6.10, 6.22, 6.36, 6.50, 7.0, 7.10, 7.30, 7.41, 7.51, 8.0, 8.15, 8.28, 8.43, 8.57, 9.5 a.m. AFTER 9.5 a.m. EVERY SEVEN MINUTES until 6.37 p.m., then 6.44, 6.52, 6.59, 7.6, 7.20, 7.35, 7.42, 7.50, 8.5, 8.12, 8.20, 8.29, 8.41 p.m. AFTER 8.41 p.m. EVERY TEN MINUTES until 11.34 p.m. |
| **LAWRENCE HILL** (G.W.R) for HANHAM. | 5.33, 5.52, 6.3, 6.10, 6.18, 6.30, 6.44, 6.58, 7.8, 7.18, 7.38, 7.49, 7.59, 8.8, 8.23, 8.36, 8.51, 9.5, 9.13 a.m. AFTER 9.13 a.m. EVERY SEVEN MINUTES until 6.45 p.m., then 6.52, 7.0, 7.7, 7.14, 7.28, 7.43, 7.50, 7.58, 8.13, 8.20, 8.28, 8.37, 8.49 p.m. AFTER 8.49 p.m. EVERY TEN MINUTES until 11.18 p.m. |
| **ST. GEORGE** (Bath Road Junction) for HANHAM. | 4.59, 5.5, 5.13, 5.18, 5.33, 5.41, 6.0, 6.11, 6.18, 6.23, 6.38, 6.52, 7.6, 7.16, 7.23, 7.46, 7.57, 8.7, 8.16, 8.31, 8.44, 8.59, 9.13, 9.21 a.m. AFTER 9.21 a.m. EVERY SEVEN MINUTES until 6.53 p.m., then 7.0, 7.6, 7.15, 7.22, 7.36, 7.51, 7.58, 8.3, 8.21, 8.28, 8.36, 8.45, 8.57 p.m. AFTER 8.57 p.m. EVERY TEN MINUTES until 11.26 p.m. |
| **MARLING ROAD** for HANHAM. | 5.2, 5.8, 5.15, 5.21, 5.36, 5.44, 6.3, 6.14, 6.21, 6.29, 6.41, 6.55, 7.9, 7.19, 7.29, 7.49, 8.0, 8.10, 8.19, 8.34, 8.47, 9.2, 9.16, 9.24 a.m. AFTER 9.24 a.m. EVERY SEVEN MINUTES until 6.56 p.m., then 7.3, 7.11, 7.18, 7.25, 7.39, 7.54, 8.1, 8.9, 8.24, 8.31, 8.39, 8.48, 9.0 p.m. AFTER 9.0 p.m. EVERY TEN MINUTES until 11.29 p.m. |

**SATURDAYS.**—AFTER MID-DAY ADDITIONAL CARS ARE RUN AND THE ACCELERATED SERVICE CONTINUES UP TO THE LAST CARS.

**SUNDAYS.**—CARS RUN EVERY FEW MINUTES BETWEEN BUSHY PARK AND HANHAM.

| | | First | | Last | | |
|---|---|---|---|---|---|---|
| HANHAM FOR OLD MARKET AND BUSHY PARK | ... | 2.21 p.m. | ,, | 9.34 p.m. | ... | To Old Market only, 10.5 p.m. |
| MARLING ROAD FOR OLD MARKET AND BUSHY PARK | ... | 2.29 p.m. | ,, | 9.42 p.m. | | |
| ST. GEORGE FOR OLD MARKET AND BUSHY PARK | ... | 2.0 p.m. | ,, | 9.45 p.m. | ,, ,, | 10.13 p.m. |
| VICTORIA ROAD FOR OLD MARKET AND BUSHY PARK | ... | 2.4 p.m. | ,, | 9.49 p.m. | ,, ,, | 10.12 p.m. |
| LAWRENCE HILL FOR OLD MARKET AND BUSHY PARK | ... | 2.8 p.m. | ,, | 9.53 p.m. | ,, ,, | 10.16 p.m. |
| OLD MARKET FOR JOINT STATION AND BUSHY PARK | ... | 2.17 p.m. | ,, | 10.1 p.m. | | |
| BUSHY PARK TO OLD MARKET AND HANHAM | ... | 2.32 p.m. | ,, | 9.47 p.m. | To Marling Road only, 10.17 p.m. |
| OLD MARKET TO HANHAM | ... | 2.20 p.m. | ,, | 10.2 p.m. | | |
| LAWRENCE HILL TO HANHAM | ... | 2.26 p.m. | ,, | 10.10 p.m. | ,, ,, | 10.40 p.m. |
| VICTORIA ROAD TO HANHAM | ... | 2.32 p.m. | ,, | 10.14 p.m. | ,, ,, | 10.44 p.m. |
| ST. GEORGE TO HANHAM | ... | 2.6 p.m. | ,, | 10.18 p.m. | | |
| MARLING ROAD TO HANHAM | ... | 2.9 p.m. | ,, | 10.21 p.m. | | |

In addition to the above service THE KINGSWOOD CARS run both WEEK DAYS and SUNDAYS BETWEEN ST. GEORGE (Bath Road Junction) AND OLD MARKET, giving a frequent service of cars between OLD MARKET and ST. GEORGE.

## WORKMEN'S CARS AND FARES.

All Cars arriving at OLD MARKET and HANHAM TERMINI before 8 a.m., carry BONA-FIDE WORKPEOPLE (i.e., Artisans, Mechanics and Daily Labourers) at the reduced Workmen's Fares, and in the evening the undermentioned cars. Workmen travelling by cars other than these will be charged the Full Ordinary Fare and Passengers other than bona-fide Workmen travelling by Workmen's Cars will also be charged the Full Ordinary Fare. The Company, however, reserve to themselves the right to refuse to carry on any Workmen's Cars passengers who are not bona-fide Workpeople. The Workmen's Cars (morning and evening, every week day) are distinguished by a board across the window over the platform at each end of the car, lettered "WORKMEN'S CAR."

SMOKING. PASSENGERS ARE REQUESTED NOT TO SMOKE ON THE TWO FRONT ROWS OF SEATS ON THE OUTSIDE OF CARS.

## FARES (either way):

| | | | | | |
|---|---|---|---|---|---|
| HANHAM and MARLING ROAD | ... | 1d. | MARLING ROAD and OLD MARKET | ... ... | 2d. |
| MARLING ROAD and LAWRENCE HILL (G.W.R.) | ... | 1d. | VICTORIA ROAD and BUSHY PARK | ... ... | 2d. |
| VICTORIA ROAD (Redfield) and OLD MARKET | ... | 1d. | HANHAM and OLD MARKET | ... ... | 3d. |
| OLD MARKET (Castle St. end) and BUSHY PARK | ... | 1d. | MARLING ROAD and BUSHY PARK | ... ... | 3d. |
| HANHAM and LAWRENCE HILL (G.W.R.) | ... | 2d. | HANHAM and BUSHY PARK | ... ... | 4d. |

Passengers should receive tickets, punched in their presence by the Conductor, upon payment of fare, and the tickets must be produced or delivered up by the passenger on demand of any official of the Company.

CHILDREN above the age of Three years, whether occupying a seat or not, are charged the FULL FARE. PERAMBULATORS, MAIL CARTS and ORDINARY BICYCLES are carried on the front platform of the Car when convenient, and only when accompanied by passengers, and at owner's risk, the

14) Having walked in from Longwell Green the pleasant sight of the terminus with the Bristol tram waiting to take you into town. Bences bus on the Hanham to Staple Hill route alongside the two cyclists make up the full extent of the traffic. What a contrast to today. The Baptist Chapel on right, c.1920.

15) Hanham terminus with tram for Bushy Park having just left. One parked car, the petrol tanker and one horse and cart almost create a traffic jam. The Welcome cafe and store on right. BP petrol for sale.

16) Tram car 199 not long out from the manufacturers workshop looking resplendent poses with its immaculate looking crew at the Hanham terminus. Note route details written along band over window c.1901.

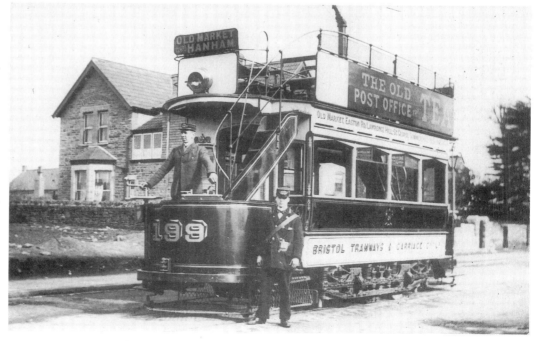

17) Sister car 198 leaves the terminus bound for Old Market on a sunny afternoon. A group of local residents stroll around without needing the safety of the pavement. Bences Motor Bus Garage on left. c.1925

18 & 19

Tram car 139 waiting at the terminus for its return journey to Old Market. Albion van GP9028 on left, no other vehicles in sight. 17th April 1939.

Sample workman's return ticket. c.1925

20) Are you sure this is as far as you go? Destination blind already changed for the return journey. Victoria Road left of tram. Note the change in livery compared with car 199. W.S. Hunter chemist shop in background. Picture taken during 1938.

21) Children on way home from Creswick Avenue School. Victoria Road on right. Pound Chapel centre background c.1930.

22) Car 192 at the end of its journey having just passed sister car 194 on its way to Knowle. Summer white caps worn by crew. Victoria Road on right, Pound Chapel in background. c.1938.

23) Car 200 on final leg of its journey from Bushy Park on a bright sunny afternoon. Horse traffic still predominates. c.1914

24) Car 189 in from Bushy Park on a quiet summer's afternoon. A small group has gathered to watch the photographer. Card postally used on 23rd December 1918 as a Christmas card.

25) From corner of Chapel Road looking back up the High Street towards terminus. Youngsters have no fear of playing in the street, c,1925

26) A similar view to the previous one but this was probably taken ten years earlier. Percy A. Bull advertises his grocers shop on the blind. Chapel Road off to left. Tram at terminus c.1915.

27) Couple wait at tram stop, solitary car parked on bend in background, deliveries by horse and cart at junction with Lower Hanham Road, c.1920.

28) Car 121 on its way into town passing the Crown & Horseshoe. Extension built 1901 on right with the gardens of Nursery Villas on left. Young lady walks happily across an empty High Street. A peaceful scene c.1910.

29) Car 192 climbing the last part of Bryant's Hill about to pass Tabernacle Road on right and Church Road on left. Porched building is the local station of the Gloucestershire Constabulary. Roger Ales advertised about shop. c.1905.

78. Hanham, Bristol.

BRYANT'S HILL ROAD.

30) An empty Bryant's Hill on a sunny early morning around 1920. Albert Henry Dumble trades at 176 as a saddler. Right at the end of the city boundary. Note crossover which enabled outward trams to run back to Beaconsfield Road depot without having to continue into Hanham.

31) Drivers view as tram heads up Bryant's Hill on way to Old Market. Mullins grocery shop on left with delivery bike parked outside. Two vehicles stand outside shops on right. One other car makes up the full extent of the traffic c.1925.

BRYANTS HILL ST. GEORGE.                                    A7432.

32) Not a tram in sight. However, this would have been the view that would have greeted you had you got off the tram in the previous picture and turned into Church Road. Group of houses known locally as Mud Rank. c.1930.

33) Our of the dip car 193 is about to ascent Bryant's Hill. On its shortened journey to Old Market it passes a prominent Wincarnis advertisement and with two cars in background this implies another quiet day. Picture taken on the 17th April 1939.

34) On reaching Nags Head Hill the track was singled as it swept over the highest part of the route. Old cottage on right. Harcourt Avenue off to the left. c.1936.

35) Further along Nags Head Hill, I.J. Payne hardware shop selling coal, coke and oil as well as Colman's Mustard. Gas street lighting. St. Aidan's church pokes over the houses. c.1920.

36) Looking back along Nag's Head Hill from Firtree Lane. Double track in existence again. Note Tram Stop right on bend. c.1920.

37) Car 124 waiting to see if there are any passengers at Firtree Lane stop as none appear to be on board. This shows the last standard livery adopted by the tramway company. When the picture was taken on 17th April 1939 the end of the system was already being discussed.

38) Four months later car 200 with slightly more passengers on board descends Nag's Head Hill behind a Morris car about to pass the Horse & Jockey selling Simonds Stout. FAE 431 parked on right. Picture taken 21st August 1939. Note track merging into one.

39) An early shot looking back up Nag's Head Hill past the Lord Raglan selling Bristol United Ales & Stouts. Note double track and ornate post in contrast to gas lamp on left. No houses on right, a much more rural scene than today. c.1905.

40) A large group pose for the cameraman in front of F. Marshall's shop as the track tops, the brow of Air Balloon Hill. Alsop's furniture is sold at 59 Broadmead, Bristol c.1905.

41) As Summerhill Road narrows the track system was again singled but before reaching the fountain double track was again introduced. Car 150 on route to Old Market during 21st August 1939.

42) With a change in the weather bringing a summer shower, Car 200 (see also picture 38) has reached the Fountain and the junction with the Kingswood line on the 21st August 1939.

43) Car 163 outward bound to Hanham, passes sister car 166 on her way to Old Market. More summer showers mean that the Driver of 163 looks more like a fisherman in his sou' wester than a tram driver. Picture taken 4 August 1939.

44) An interior view of the Beaconsfield Road Depot, built during 1876. Two new electric tram cars 161 and 88 housed for the opening of the Kingswood route. Horse drawn tram, with 7 windows and now to be used as a trailer can be seen on the right. Picture probably taken around September 1895.

*(See also last picture of Part 3)*

45) An unidentified tram about to leave the Beaconsfield Road Depot, to start the Hanham to Knowle route. An identical enamel advertising panel for Anderson's Waterproof can be seen in a private yard in Braggs Lane, Old Market. Pipe tobacco advertised at 8d (3p) per ounce. c.1939.

46) Just about to join the main line, car 135 emerges from Beaconsfield Road on its way down to Old Market. Toddler with pram on right, long shadows and the spring sunshine add to this interesting picture. 17 April 1939.

47) Car 150 just out of the Beaconsfield Road Depot, on a damp morning about to start the short working service to Old Market. Bristol East Labour Headquarters on left (no pun intended!!) 4 August 1939

48) Although the two pictures on this page of Church Road, Redfield, are the same, they have both been included as they each show individual interesting features. Here the interlacing track can be clearly seen, together with a full shot of the St. George Police Station.

49) This view shows part of the yard of Frederick Summers Monumental Masons, with De Reszke cigarettes being advertised. Parked on the left is a van AHU 382, ready to deliver sand and cement anywhere in the area. Car 113 is working the Nag's Head Hill (Top) service, and has stopped to allow passengers to get off. 169 has been waiting for clearance before proceeding on into the interlaced track section on its way to Old Market. 17 April 1939

50) A much earlier picture of Church Road Redfield. R.H. Cox & Son are the monumental masons for the Avon View Cemetery. Horse drawn traffic predominates, tram in background just coming around bend. Young man with hand-cart on left. A lot quieter than today, all of the buildings shown are still with us. Taken from a card postally used in 1906. Picture c.1904.

51) Car 17 leaves this section of interlaced track, whilst working the Kingswood to Tramway Centre service, on a bright sunny day. Seven motor cars in picture, buildings very similar today. 17 April 1939.

52) St. George's School in a semi-rural scene, which includes a cart load of hay coming down the hill. Edwardian dressed lady on right. John Hy. Williams, farrier on left with horse patiently waiting to be shod. c.1905.

53) Car 124 has travelled further down Church Road on its way to Old Market. The White Lion public house is on the left, whilst just further up the road is the Albert Inn. Off right is Worsley Street. A rather tranquil scene, not a bit like today, and WW2 is less than a month away. 4 August 1939.

54) St. Lawrence's Church pokes up over the Co-operative buildings, home to the Bristol & District Co-operative Society Ltd., and C.W. Cook Scale Makers.

Berkeley Street is off to the right, and in front there is a good example of a central trolley pole, stretching over the double track. Compare this with the side pole on the left with its bracketed arm covering both tracks. c.1904.

55) Car 187 breasts the top of the hump over the Great Western Railway lines at Lawrence Hill, as it passes Pugsley & Sons Ltd., premises. 17 April 1939.

56) On a rather wet summers day, car 53 is seen on its way to Marling Road, running up behind an unidentified tram, as it passes car 200 working down to Old Market. Note lorry HD 6394 on left with 20 m.p.h. plate at the rear. Morton Street and Thomas Street run off to the right, tower of Christ Church, Cobden Street stands above the surrounding buildings. 4 August 1939

57) Car 136 runs over the junction with the Eastville/Staple Hill route, as it enters West Street from Clarence Road, on route to the Tramway Centre from Kingswood. Van HY 8547 is seen passing a Rolls Royce EUU 237. 21 August 1939.

58) A general view of Old Market Street during the first decade of the twentieth century. Empire & Hippodrome on right with Frederick G. Cullingford's grocery and wine store next door. Gabled houses in between, then the clock over the Bristol Tramway & Carriage Office can be seen. Car 198 is about to leave for Nag's Head Hill (Top). Castle Street can be seen in centre background. c.1905.

59) A more modern view of Old Market Street, with Tower Lane off to the left. Foster's Corner at junction with Castle Street as it continues on behind tram car 34 on its way to Zetland Road, from Eastville. Shops on right hand side are: Olivers, Cliftons, Groves Radio, and 50 Shilling Tailors. 28 December 1938.

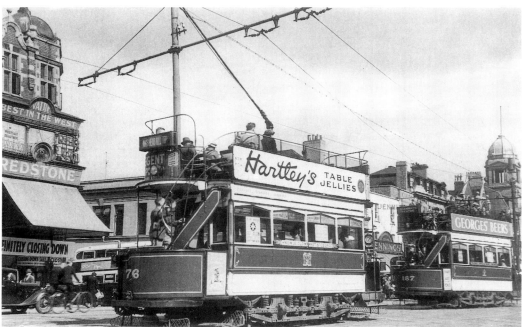

60) Tram No.76 is working the short service to Nag's Head Hill (Top), and is just about to pass car 187 running through to the Tramway Centre, at the junction with Carey's Lane. The dome of the Central Hall is seen on the extreme right, Empire Theatre is on the left. Parson's clock is just visible in front of 76. 10 September 1937.

61) On a damp day in March 1932, Old Market shows just how busy it could be as a tram terminus and through route (only second to the Tramway Centre). Car 146 is ready to work the service to Staple Hill, once the unidentified tram gets out of the way. Tram 174 is on the clear road to allow it to continue through to the Centre from Kingswood. No.23 will take the short trip to Marling Road, and stands behind a car about to leave for Hanham. 29 March 1932.

62) Shortly after tram car 174 passed through the congestion, No.24 arrived en route to Zetland Road. Here it has been captured on camera standing alongside its stable mate No.23. 29 March 1932.

63) Old Market Street in the 1920's with car 160 working service 14 to Staple Hill. Behind and to the left can be seen the Empire Theatre, the Kings Cinema, and the Central Hall. On the right car 122 is working route 15, St. George to Bushy Park, and stands in front of the Stag & Hounds, one of the few buildings seen in this picture that is still with us. c.1924/25.

64 ) Trio of cars in Old Market with 89 getting ready for Kingswood, 188 running through to the Tramway Centre on its way from Kingswood, and tram 126 picking up passengers for Hanham. The Kings Cinema and the Central Hall are on the left. 28 December 1938.

65) Policeman watching the cameraman, around 1912, tram for Eastville, from Durdham Downs, whilst on the same route is car 18. On the right can be seen car 188 which is working through from Kingswood to the Tramway Centre. c.1912.

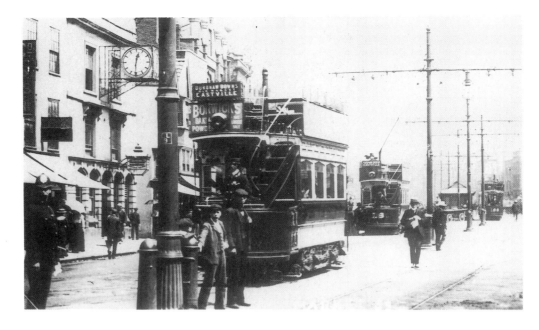

66) Looking down on to a busy Old Market Street full of interesting features including two solid tyre single deck buses (AE 2552 on route 31). Car 132 in background on route 14 to Durdham Downs. On left car 158 has a full load for Staple Hill. 197 on centre back is half way through the run from Bushy Park to Hanham with a Kingswood bound tram in front. Car 114 is working route 15 Hanham to Bushy Park. Taken at 5.44 p.m. on an August evening in 1916.

Old Market St., Bristol. 1446.

67) Old Market Street from a slightly different angle. Cars 3, 181 and 118 plus an unidentified tram visible on the Eastville, Kingswood and Hanham routes. Factory chimneys dominate the skyline. Two newspaper boys are seen centre picture. All other vehicles seen are of the horsedrawn variety. c.1905.

Old Market Street, Bristol.

68) Old Market from top of car 141 (the old Directors' car) en route to Staple Hill. Cars 91 and 146 in front, car 166 about to leave for Nag's Head Hill (Top). 6 April 1938.

69) 164 stands opposite the Bata Shoe Shop in Old Market on its way to Knowle. 21 August 1938

70) "The Hanham Tram 1900" is the title of this picture. Unfortunately the exact location is uncertain and the names of the crew are unknown.

71) Almost mid-day in high summer. Peace has returned, the depression has not yet started. Car 29 on route 3 to Durdham Downs, whilst car 174 is working route 13 Old Market to Kingswood. Hornby's Dairies Ltd. van on left. Policeman with ornate helmet. Stag & Hounds on right. All other buildings now gone. c.1921.

72) Taken from a coloured card postally used 15 January 1907. As it was printed in London tram car 152 is coloured red and cream, rather than blue and cream. The tram is about to swing right into Tower Lane on its way to Bushy Park. Lower Castle Street off to the left. Edwardian ladies in their finery. c.1910.

73) In the Spring sunshine a group of ladies walk indian file around pavement work outside the Empire Theatre. Car 113 is resting awhile before it continues on to Knowle. In the background car 17 is on its way to Eastville whilst no. 75 is off to Hanham. Carey's Lane can be seen on the left, opposite is the Stag & Hounds Public House, one of the few buildings in existence today. 6 April 1938.

74) A poor quality, but nevertheless interesting, photograph taken around 1908. Car 112 to Kingswood, whilst No. 152 will shortly swing round into Tower Lane on its way to Bushy Park.

75) Having left Old Market, car 198 continues route 15 down Tower Hill towards Passage Street and over St. Philips Bridge. Sign on left advertises a Shellfish and Oyster Bar whilst on the right Blakes advertise hygienic appliances for sale. c.1925.

76) On to Knowle with original destination blind on right. Part of Peter Davey's collection.

77) Car 114 is seen crossing "Ha'penny Bridge" (St. Philips) on route 15 Hanham/Bushy Park behind a War Department Tractor. Note length of steering linkage and size of radiator. c.1917.

78) Construction of the Counterslip Power House. 7 May 1900.

79) The finished building. c.1902.

80) The same junction showing the complexity of the track with traffic from the Centre coming over Bristol bridge crossing the lines which connected Bath Street and Redcliffe Street (not used as any part of a service route) c.1908.

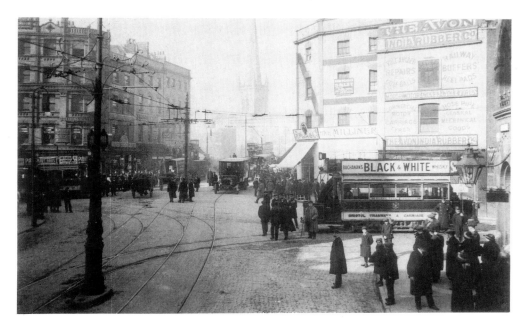

81) This is a BTCC publicity shot showing an unidentified tram car having turned into Bath Street from Victoria Street on its way from Bushy Park to Hanham. Note single track in Bath Street and because of the angle of the road trams heading to Knowle would have to go around the Standard on to the wrong line before switching to their own track behind camera. c.1914.

82) Looking back along Victoria Road towards Temple Meads Reynolds Hotel on left has recently been rebuilt in the same style following war damage. Nearly all other buildings lost either in the Blitz or to progress. From a card postally used 18 November 1906.

83) Victoria Street with horsedrawn tram just about to go out of shot bottom right hand corner. Temple Street and Church Lane off to the right, Mitchell Lane left foreground. Most of the buildings were lost in the War, but the leaning Tower of Temple Church fortunately remains with us. c.1902.

84) Victoria Street from ground level with car 227 working through to Hanham passing Avon Street on the right. c.1905.

85) Temple Gate showing 4 trams on the Brislington and Knowle routes with car 24 heading for Hanham. In the centre of the picture is a car coming out of the Temple Meads Joint Station Tram Shed. Almost certainly another BTCC posed picture. c.1905.

86) Looking back past Temple Gate towards Victoria Street. Single decker bus working route 23. Another BTCC posed photograph, c.1905.

87) I'll let you go first!! Car 208 leaves the Tram Shed en route to the Tramway Centre whilst the car on the right is on its way to Hanham. c.1905.

88) Car 207 negotiates the complexity of the track at the Victoria St/Bath St. junction on its way to Brislington, followed by a single decker bus. Lord Mayor's car on right? Note policeman on point duty. 1st May 1934.

89) Above, car 204 emerging from the Tram Shed at Temple Meads Joint Station. This track can still be seen on the left of the incline. c.1905.

90) Car 68 working the Knowle to Bristol bridge route whilst behind 208 works route 8, c.1910.

91) Pass along inside, still more people to get on!! Car 152 on its way to Knowle at the bottom of the railway station incline. 12 August 1938.

92) Bath Bridge looking back to Temple Gate. Trams vie for road space with three horse carts and one cyclist. The Castle and Plough Inn stands on the corner of Clarence Road. c.1911.

93) Horse drawn tram at the Three Lamps. c.1890.

94) A close up of The Three Lamps, horsepower still very much in evidence. Roger's Page Ale advertised. Tree on right spreads over towards the Tram wires. c.1910.

95) The junction of Bath Road and Wells Road. Tram on its way to Bushy Park in the background. All these buildings and high wall on the right were swept away for road improvements. c.1911.

96) A similar view to the previous with two Trams on the Knowle, Bristol Bridge, Hanham routes. Note "points boy" in centre with his rod to enable him to manually change the points. c.1920.

97) The picture is entitled Tram Junction, Totterdown and was for some while the terminal point of the line before it was extended to The Red Lion at Knowle. Cars 72 and 68 operate route 10 Knowle to Bristol Bridge. Pedestrians feel quite happy to stand in the road, particularly the two young men who are idly watching the cameraman, c.1914.

98) World War 1 had occurred between the taking of this and the previous picture with little change to the buildings. Tram 67 is also working route 10 to Bristol Bridge. c.1920.

99) A similar view looking up Wells Road, almost thirty years after the previous picture. Car 157 is returning to Hanham having passed No.71 on its way to Knowle. Signpost directs you along the B3120 to Bridgwater, c.1933.

100) Bushy Park, the original terminus of the route from Hanham. Totterdown YMCA dominates the area. Bullock's Mineral Water being delivered on the left. Car 10 heads towards Old Market and on out to Hanham, c.1905.

101) Car 80 is captured at Bushy Park by the camera during the last month of tram services operating from Knowle. The Driver is wrapped up against the wet weather. Hodders the Chemist are in the rank of shops behind the tram. Headline board reads "Terms of Soviet Japanese Armistice". 12 August 1938

102) Looking back across the "Bush" towards the City. W. Goodall & Sons advertise on the sun blind their home-made Boots & Shoes. Pedestrians chat and stroll around in the Summer sunshine. Car 67 works its way to Knowle, c.1905.

103) A view looking in the opposite direction, as the hill continues to climb towards Knowle. Advertisement for Snowball Patent Flour dominates the scene whilst the cameraman has caught the attention of a number of interested people. c.1912.

63

104) Further along Wells Road looking down the hill towards the "Bush" from Firfield Street. Delivery cart on right. Car 120 on its way to Knowle. c.1912.

105) Some 16 years later a similar view shows that a number of houses on the right have now been converted into shops. Car 73 passes a MacKay's delivery van registration mark AE 8260. Man on right has a hard job pulling his hand cart up the hill. Beer barrels being conveyed by horse power on left. c.1920.

106) Wells Road at its junction with Clyde Road. Tram on its way back into the City. Most of the buildings remain today. Taken from a card postally used in 1904.

107) A similar view of Wells road looking towards the City Centre. School Road off to the right. The only vehicular traffic in this picture is one horsedrawn van. Somewhat different to today. Note ornate Street Lamp and Standard. c.1910.

108) Car 69 sweeps down past Holy Nativity Church on its way to Bristol Bridge on a bright Summers day whilst opposite, young boy pushes his bike up the Hill. c.1910

109) Looking back down Wells Road as car 70 struggles up the hill. Very much as today but without the tram and tram tracks and with the small trees very much more matured. Taken from a card posted 22 January 1908.

110) Car 131 stops to pick up passengers outside the Totterdown Hotel on its way up the hill to Knowle. 12 August 1938.

111) Car 208 is about to take the plunge down the long hill to Totterdown on its way to Bristol Bridge. Pony and trap and The George Inn are on the right. Three boys pose for the cameraman. Note that standing on the platform of the tram is a "clippie", one of the few select bands of women who became Conductresses in 1916. Picture taken in 1918.

112) Still climbing Wells Road Hill is car 72 having travelled through from Hanham. Belluton Road is on the left. c.1910.

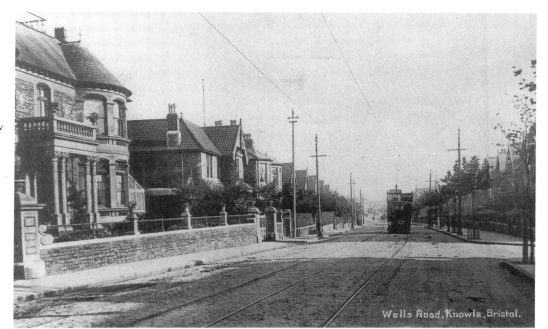

113) Car 73 appears to be the only moving object in this view of Wells Road. The elegant double bay villa on the left is now Cleeve House School. Woodridge Road off on the right. c.1935.

114) Car 133 has climbed away from the City where a short while previously there had been a heavy summer storm, hence the reason for the tram's headlight being switched on. Driver checking that all of the passengers have got on. One car and three cyclists add to the density of the traffic. 12 August 1938.

115) Car 214 passes Redcatch Road with the Wesleyan Chapel on the corner having been "seen off" by the large black dog. Greenmore Road is off to the right with a rank of shops facing Wells Road. Taken from card postally used 13 April 1911.

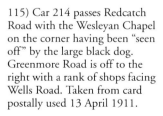

116) Wells Road looking North (back into the City). On the right is the Talbot Inn, with the adjacent cottages having now been converted into shops. Note tram tracks merge into a single track bottom left-hand corner. Only horsedrawn traffic shown in the picture. c.1905.

117) A few years later the Talbot Inn has lost its name board and gained flower boxes above the bay windows. Still looking rural. Around 1908.

118) Another view of the Talbot Inn, this time looking away from the City. Horsedrawn traffic and young children make up this interesting picture. c.1905.

119) Car 70 has just left the Knowle Terminus heading for Bristol Bridge. Most of the buildings still remain today. St. Martins Road off to the left. c.1916.

120) Wells Road junction with Priory Road, Broad Walk on the right (just out of view). Young girl in her summer frock with mother checking baby in pram. Behind her set in the wall and carved out of the masonry is the name "Woodleigh". c.1910.

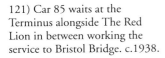

121) Car 85 waits at the Terminus alongside The Red Lion in between working the service to Bristol Bridge. c.1938.

122) Just along from the Terminus car 48 rests in between working the Knowle to Bristol Bridge route. Note learner car behind and also another interesting Aspro advertisement which suggests that they are good for irritable husbands as they sooth the nerves. 12 August 1938.

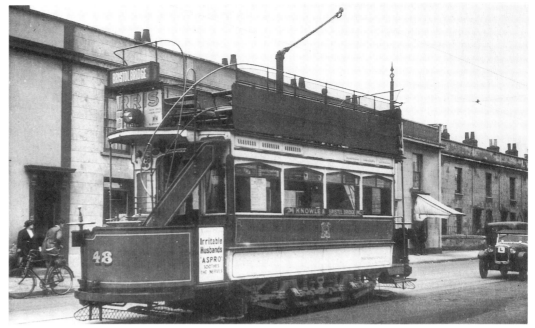

123) On a rather wet day cars 70 and 192 wait at The Red Lion Terminus on the Bristol Bridge and Hanham routes respectively. Both appropriately sport Anderson's Rubber Raincoats adverts, 29 March 1932.

124) The Red Lion Terminus track ends just in front of the Morris van AHT 983 with car 169 on the Hanham route and nearest the camera No.73 working the Bristol Bridge service. 14 July 1938.

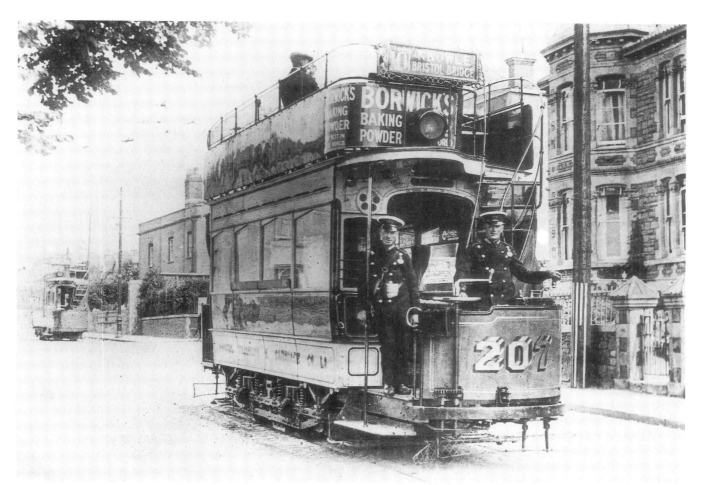

125) Car 207 stands in all its glory near to the Knowle Terminus. Both Conductor and Driver pose for the photographer whilst on top a passenger enjoys a spot of sunbathing. c.1927.

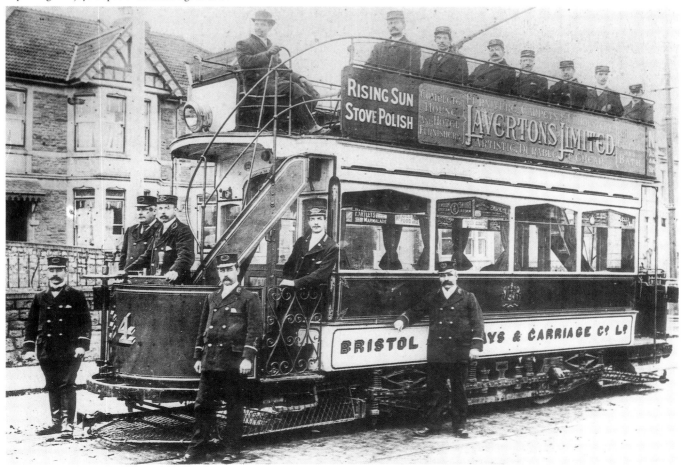

126) An official BTCC posed photograph of car 64 taken in Wells Road with some senior members of the Management Staff in their immaculate dress and nearly all sporting a well groomed moustache. c.1904.

127) Crew of 169 pose for the cameraman whilst waiting at The Red Lion, Knowle Terminus. Note open field in centre background now covered by the houses of Hengrove and Whitchurch. July 1938.

128) The Driver is getting ready to take car 133 back to Hanham from the Knowle Terminus. c.1938.

# PART 3

# THE JOURNEY

# RETURN

# TO KINGSWOOD

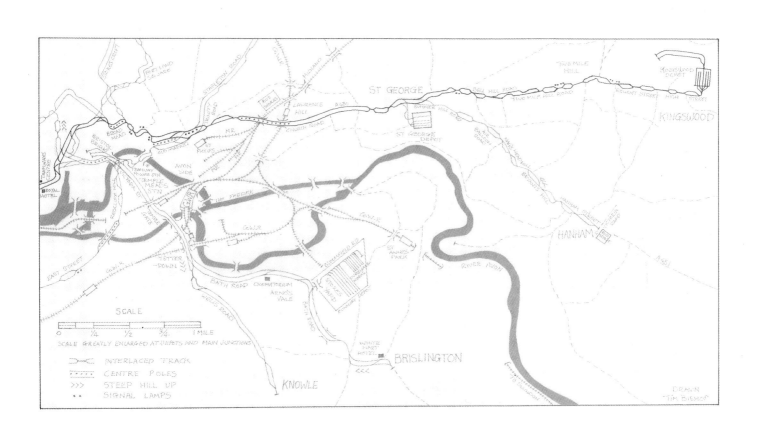

# Bristol Tramways & Carriage Company

## LIMITED.

# COMPLETE LIST OF CAR FARES.

## *Either way between the following points:*

### Tramways Centre and Durdham Downs.
#### (*Via* WHITELADIES ROAD).

| | |
|---|---|
| Tramways Centre and Tyndall's Park Road ... | 1d |
| Park Street and Durdham Downs ... ... | 1d |
| Tramways Centre and Durdham Downs ... | 2d |

### Tramways Centre and Durdham Downs.
#### (*Via* ZETLAND ROAD).

| | |
|---|---|
| Tramways Centre and Zetland Road Junction ... | 1d |
| Zetland Road Junction and Durdham Downs ... | 1d |
| Tramways Centre and Durdham Downs ... | 2d |

### Tramways Centre and Horfield.

| | |
|---|---|
| Tramways Centre and Zetland Road Junction ... | 1d |
| Zetland Road Junction and Horfield ... ... | 1d |
| Tramways Centre and Horfield ... ... | 2d |

### Tramways Centre and Fishponds.
#### (*Via* CITY ROAD).

| | |
|---|---|
| Tramways Centre and Warwick Road Junction | 1d |
| Warwick Road Junc. and Fishponds (Station Road) | 1d |
| Tramways Centre and Fishponds (Station Road). | 2d |

### Tramways Centre and Hanham.

| | |
|---|---|
| Tramways Centre and Old Market ... ... | 1d |
| Old Market and Victoria Road (Redfield) ... | 1d |
| Lawrence Hill (G.W.R.) and Marling Road ... | 1d |
| Marling Road and Hanham ... ... | 1d |
| Tramways Centre and Victoria Road (Redfield) | 2d |
| Old Market and Marling Road ... ... | 2d |
| Lawrence Hill (G.W.R.) and Hanham ... | 2d |
| Tramways Centre and Marling Road ... | 3d |
| Old Market and Hanham ... ... | 3d |
| Tramways Centre and Hanham ... ... | 4d |

### Brislington and Hotwells.

| | |
|---|---|
| Brislington and Wells Road Junction ... ... | 1d |
| Arnos Vale (Cemetery Gates) and Tramways Centre | 1d |
| Tramways Centre and Hotwells ... ... | 1d |
| Brislington and Tramways Centre ... | 2d |
| Arnos Vale (Cemetery Gates) and Hotwells ... | 2d |
| Brislington and Hotwells ... ... | 3d |

### Zetland Road and Staple Hill.

| | |
|---|---|
| Zetland Road Junc. and Old Market (Castle St. end) | 1d |
| Old Market Junction and Eastville Junction ... | 1d |
| Warwick Road Junc. and Fishponds (Station Road) | 1d |
| Fishponds (Station Road) and Staple Hill ... | 1d |
| Zetland Road Junction and Eastville Junction ... | 2d |
| Old Market and Fishponds (Station Road) ... | 2d |
| Warwick Road Junction and Staple Hill ... | 2d |
| Zetland Road Junc. and Fishponds (Station Road) | 3d |
| Old Market and Staple Hill ... ... | 3d |
| Zetland Road Junction and Staple Hill ... | 4d |

### Eastville and Durdham Downs.

| | |
|---|---|
| Eastville Junction and Old Market ... ... | 1d |
| Old Market (Castle St. end) and Tyndall's Park Road | 1d |
| Park Street and Durdham Downs ... ... | 1d |
| Eastville Junction and Tyndall's Park Road ... | 2d |
| Old Market (Castle St. end) and Durdham Downs | 2d |
| Eastville Junction and Durdham Downs ... | 3d |

### Old Market and Kingswood.

| | |
|---|---|
| Old Market and Victoria Road (Redfield) ... | 1d |
| Lawrence Hill (G.W.R.) and Whiteway Road ... | 1d |
| Whiteway Road and Kingswood ... ... | 1d |
| Old Market and Whiteway Road ... ... | 2d |
| Lawrence Hill (G.W.R.) and Kingswood ... | 2d |
| Old Market and Kingswood ... ... | 3d |

### Old Market and Bushy Park.

| | |
|---|---|
| Old Market and Bushy Park ... ... | 1d |

### Bristol Bridge and Knowle.

| | |
|---|---|
| Bristol Bridge and Bushy Park ... ... | 1d |
| Wells Road Junction and Knowle ... ... | 1d |
| Bristol Bridge and Knowle ... ... | 2d |

### Bristol Bridge and Ashton Park.

| | |
|---|---|
| Bristol Bridge (Redcliffe Street) and Ashton Park | 1d |

### Bristol Bridge and Bedminster Down.

| | |
|---|---|
| Bristol Bridge (Redcliffe St.) and Bedminster Down | 1d |

129) A general view of the Tramway Centre showing the new Hippodrome, with the half spire and globe on top. Car 232 stops en route to Hotwells, while opposite two taxi drivers in their Company uniforms stand by motor cab AE 1876. Young Edwardian Lady strolls in the sunshine whilst just above her head, on the lamp/tram standard is a small two-faced clock. c.1912.

130) The Tramway Centre, a purpose built triangular island was laid out to accommodate both the terminus of some routes, and the setting down/up of through routes. Six trams in this picture, including cars 82, 145, and 227. There are also three Blue Taxi motor cabs all with AE registrations. Note mobile hoarding on left being pushed through the streets advertising "Queen's Hall Famous Pictures". c.1911.

131) A view looking back towards Clare Street, with Picture House on the corner, and Baldwin Street in front of which is a good view of the masonry curved walls of the Drawbridge, now covered as is the rest of the River Frome, as it flows through the city. In the foreground, a single decker bus drives through on solid tyres, which together with the taxis and the trams make up this interesting composite picture, taken around 1913. From a card postally used on the 15 June 1929.

132) A more modern scene with the grace of the walls supporting the old Drawbridge still visible. Seven trams around the triangle. St. Stephen's Church Tower breaks the skyline, with the clock tower of Northcliffe House poking up on the left. c.1925.

133) Five trams nestle around the triangle with the BTCC Head Office in the background. Right hand car 129 has Fishponds as its destination. c.1934.

134) In the late spring sunshine a group of trams wait at their respective termini. From left to right 188 for Kingswood, 121 to Horfield Barracks, and 38 will soon be off to the Downs. Two buses stand in front of Radiant House, buildings behind trams now lost to modern development. May 1935.

135) With lengthening shadows cast by the afternoon sun, cars 7, 224 and 226 catch the sunshine whilst they await their passengers. 3 September 1933.

136) A general view looking towards Magpie Park with car 94 en route to Westbury, and car 211 will go to Hotwells when its crew have completed their chat!! May 1935.

137) A view looking back along Colston Avenue towards St. Mary's on the Quay. People stroll around in the winter sunshine having just enjoyed what was to become the last peaceful Christmas for six years. Car 174 has just started it journey to Kingswood. Maple Leaf coaches have their offices on left of tram. 28 December 1938.

138) Colston Avenue with St. Mary's on the Quay, Northcliffe House and Wrights the Printers buildings on the left. Skeleton of Electricity House is in the background, Taxi rank on the right. Car 114 on the final part of its journey from Kingswood. 17 April 1939.

139) Car 141 stands on the Tramway Centre en route to Fishponds, whilst alongside is No.172 working the Kingswood service. Circular disc on bulkheads are the colour coded route indicators for night-time services c.1925.

140) Car 23 leaving Colston Avenue as it enters Lewin's Mead on its way to Filton Park, and is followed by Morris registration mark FHU 261. Electricity House on right in the throes of construction. Car 58 is coming out of Rupert Street. 17 April 1939

141) Junction of Broadmead with Merchant Street. The Kingswood bound trams would come in from the left. Car 19 on its way to Zetland Road. Property on right is for sale but all buildings shown were eventually demolished to make way for Bristol's Post War development. 28 December 1938

142) On a cold wet day two cars have turned into Lower Castle Street and wait for 171 to clear the single track. 29 March 1932.

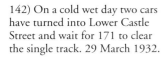

143) Peak time in Old Market. Car 182 taking its load around into Lower Castle Street, whilst cars 118, 137, 113 and 200 wait to pick up their passengers, patiently waiting in the long queues. c.1935.

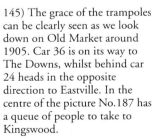

144) The early days of electrification with a three windowed electric tram towing a similarly constructed horse tram No.108. Both with a full complement of male passengers sat outside in the summer sunshine. Note letter 'K' for Kingswood on the trailer. Car 116 waits on the through road. Toilets blocks in the centre of the street. c.1897.

145) The grace of the trampoles can be clearly seen as we look down on Old Market around 1905. Car 36 is on its way to The Downs, whilst behind car 24 heads in the opposite direction to Eastville. In the centre of the picture No.187 has a queue of people to take to Kingswood.

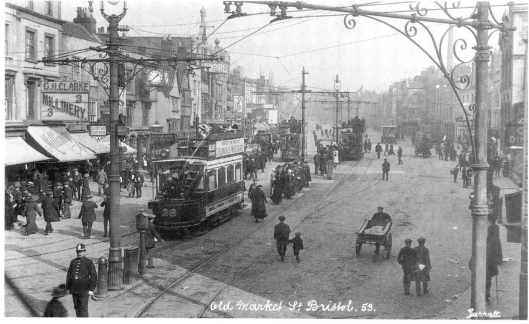

146) General view of Old Market with Eastville bound cars on left whilst on the right car 188 enters Old Market Street from Kingswood, with the driver sporting a straw boater. Taken from card postally used 15 August 1905.

147) View from the top of a tram looking back towards Castle Street, with Tower Lane on left, Lower Castle Street on the right. Car 181 about to take passengers through to the Tramway Centre. 28 December 1938.

148) Almost certainly a BTCC posed picture taken in Old Market around 1896.

149) No.216 is taken in an almost identical position to the previous picture. Empire Theatre remains the same, but the buildings on the left are new. Also new are the two Bristol K5G's double deck buses with c3208 FHT 794 on left. 21 August 1939

150) An unusual view of Old Market Street taken from a point which is now roughly the centre of a large roundabout, looking towards Castle Street. Car 113 rests before returning to Nag's Head Hill (top) whilst 236 on the right is ready to set off to Kingswood. 17 April 1939

151) 164 prepared to continue its journey to Kingswood with Carey's Lane off to the left. Newspaper poster states "(Germany) May have a military GOVT". A rather poignant statement in view of the fate awaiting this tramcar, it being totally destroyed by enemy action when a bomb fell on the entrance to Bedminster Depot in the early hours of the 4 January 1941. c.1937.

152) A similar positioned shot to the previous picture with car 14 awaiting both crew and passengers before leaving for Kingswood. No.143 however is about to set off for Hanham displaying the advertisement that "Jones are Bristol's most modern store". c.1938

153) The Christmas festivities are over and it will be another six years before there will be a peaceful. Christmas, and long before then there will be no more trams to grace Bristol's streets. Car 89 for Kingswood passes 188 on its way to the Tramway Centre, with 126 loading for Hanham. (1.52p.m.) 28 December 1938.

154) No.216 waits in Old Market before proceeding to Kingswood. 21August 1939.

Trinity Church, St Phillips, Bristol.

155) Parting of the ways. Left to Eastville, Fishponds and Staple Hill whilst on the right the lines continues along Clarence Road to Hanham and Kingswood. People strolling around both in the road and on the pavement. c.1912

156) Unfortunately, not a very good copy, but pictures of trams in Clarence Road/West Street, Old Market are so rare, it was felt necessary to include this particular view. c.1912.

Clarence Road West Street Bristol

157.) Car 12 leaves the single track section as it winds its way on route 15 through Lawrence Hill. St. Lawrence Church rises up in front of the tram. Wellesley Street off to the right, with the Wellesley Arms on the corner. c.1920.

158) Looking back towards the City end of Lawrence Hill as car 196 passes a milk cart with a group of people round it. Co-operative Building is on the right, as is the entrance to Leadhouse Road. Croydon Street has the obstacle of a lamp standard to be negotiated, hence the white paint. Charlton Street off to the left, c.1910.

159) Over the first bridge which crossed the London- Midland railway line. Packhorse Inn on the right. Children are happy to stand in the road and watch the cameraman. Tram in the distance has passed Ducie Road on its way to Kingswood. c.1910.

160) Car 53 to Nag's Head Hill (Top) runs down from the Midland Railway Bridge to the junction with Ducie Road. Earl Russell Public House on right many of the buildings in the foreground exist today. 21 August 1939.

161) Looking along Church Road, Redfield from the corner of Victoria Road. Young lady makes sure that her hat is on straight for the photographer. Post Office and S. Mead, drapers shop, behind. Hewetts Store and George & Dragon Public House on the right. Tram 182 is on its way to Hanham. Milk delivery cart heads in towards the City. c.1905.

162) Car 192 running through to Bushy Park with the St. George School dominating the centre background. Old cottages on the right by a large hoarding. Union flag hangs from the property opposite the tram. c.1902.

163) Early days in Church Road, Redfield with car 112 at the tram stop on its way to Hanham. Albert Gimblitt noted Fish Bar on the right. Victoria Road is on the left with tin baths hanging up outside George Hillier's Ironmongers shop. c.1905.

164) The St. George Fountain with 187 coming out from Clouds Hill Road being overtaken by a Ford car hoping that nothing was coming down from Summerhill Road. 17 April 1939.

165) Looking across to the Kingswood bound electric car towing a seven windowed horse car. Only male passengers would be allowed outside on the trailer as there are no decency boards fitted. c.1896.

166) Car 158 shows off its new Wartime austerity livery of blue and white, totally unlined. Bumper bars and sand boxes painted white to help out in the blackout. As it turned out, this was the only tram to be given this particular livery and was the penultimate passenger vehicle to be scrapped. June 1940.

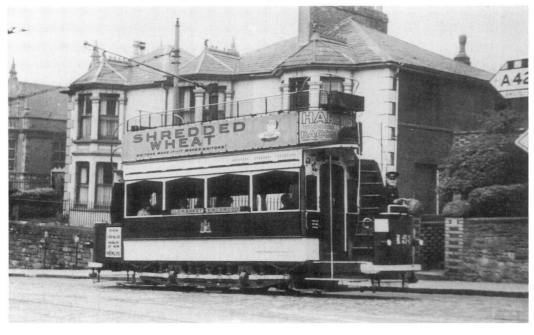

167) Clouds Hill Road looking back towards the Fountain. Car 157 traverses the interlaced section of track before regaining the double section on the long drag up to Kingswood. Nearly all the buildings seen exist today. 21 August 1939.

168) Nº135 runs through the Whiteway Road terminus past the Tramway Tavern on the left with the World's End Pub on the right to Old Market (now the end of the line, the service to the Centre having been withdrawn a short while before). 4 August 1939.

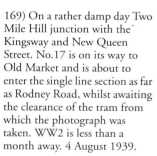

169) On a rather damp day Two Mile Hill junction with the Kingsway and New Queen Street. No.17 is on its way to Old Market and is about to enter the single line section as far as Rodney Road, whilst awaiting the clearance of the tram from which the photograph was taken. WW2 is less than a month away. 4 August 1939.

170) Car 187 in blackout paint stands in Two Mile Hill just up from the junction with New Queen Street. The decency board panel advertises "defend your City, join the 66th Searchlight regiment, 500 men urgently wanted". Whilst the gate panel recommends Aspro as relief against the heatwave. c.1940.

171) A little further up Two Mile Hill at the junction with Charlton Road car no.7 picks up passengers, with its trucks, bumpers and sand boxes painted white for blackout purposes. Note also that the window tops and the destination box have been painted black to prevent light showing at night. The heatwave relief is still obtainable from Aspro. c.1940.

172) More single track, this time being negotiated by car 36 on its way to Old Market. Zion Chapel out of picture on the left. All buildings shown still remain. 4 August 1939.

173) Regent Street looking back towards Bristol. Midland Railway Parcel's Office on the right with Street Gas Lamp in front. Picture taken from a card posted on the 17 July 1907.

174) Under the conditions of the Act of Parliament authorising the construction of the line, trams were not supposed to operate when there was a procession. Car 174 has however been caught up with this particular procession and remains stationary. c.1927.

175) Regent Street and the Jubilee Clock Tower. J.H. Mills grocers shop on the left with ornate ironwork catching the summer sunshine. c.1918.

176) The High Street showing the only descent available to the trams during their long haul up to Kingswood (300ft above Old Market). A mixture of shops including one in the centre which appears to have had an accident with its blind. The Jubilee Clock shows that it is almost 1.30 p.m. Tram car 18 in the background. c.1910.

177) Winter sunshine casts its shadows across the High Street. Holy Trinity Church stands out behind the trees. Many people are sauntering along the pavement and with just one horsecart, makes up this semi rural scene of around 1905.

178) Car 135 at the Kingswood terminus ready for the return journey to Old Market. Note the trolley arm automatic reversing triangle left of the tram. Will Hay is showing at the Regent Cinema in "Ask a Policeman". 4 August 1939.

179) The same scene, this time taken from the top of a tram waiting on the up-line. The entrance to the Kingswood Depot curves in across the road just behind the two people left of tram car 135. 4 August 1939.

180) A ground shot of Kingswood terminus showing car 86 (the new vehicle built in 1920 to replace the old car 86 converted into a rail grinder). The fate of the tramway system is very much in the balance, with many lines already closed. WW2 is just two weeks away and the threat of this War will save the Kingswood line for a short while at least. 21 August 1939

181) 126 waits at the terminus and is still working the full service through to the Tramway Centre. Single deck bus in background on its way to Wick. 4 August 1938.

182) 188 rests at the end of its journey from the Tramway Centre, whilst No 33 starts the journey down hill to the Centre by having to climb a short rise before the level of Regent Street. c.1937.

183) Car 171 just coming to the end of its journey up the long drag from Old Market. Buildings shown in the picture still remain. It is only the density of the traffic and the absence of the tram that marks the main difference with today's view. 4 August 1939.

184) A close-up of car 189 just out of the Depot, the entrance of which can be seen behind the pedestrian on the left. c.1937.

185) War time shot of the Kingswood stable showing from left to right cars 19, 216, 214 and 173 all sporting their blackout white paint. Note the young airman standing on the platform of 173 and also the sharp curves of the track needed to be negotiated in and out of the left-hand side of the Depot. c.1940.

186) View of the Kingswood Tram Shed from inside the yard. Two Inspectors, Driver and Storeman pose in front of cars 181, 182, 170, 172 and 183. 14 July 1938.

187) Five cars occupy the left-hand reserve road. The end vehicle is probably one of the Rail Grinders. First car in line is No. 132. c.1937.

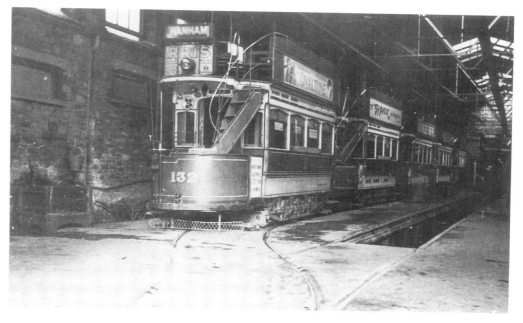

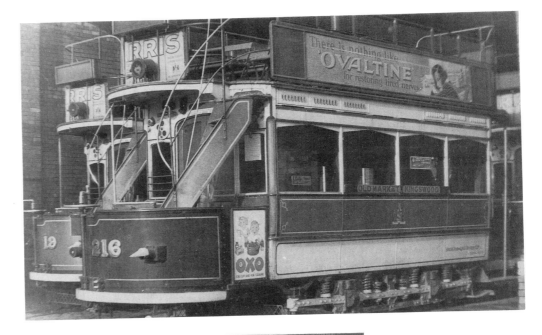

188) Cars 19 and 216 stand on the two left-hand lines of the Kingswood Depot in their War paint. Note hooded lamps and blacked out destination box. c.1940.

189) Having decided to scrap the Trams in the large field behind the Kingswood Depot, it was necessary to knock a hole in the back wall of the shed and extend the rails and trolley wires. This show shows the Grinder car standing on the scrap road, whilst car 33 has already been partly dismantled and is only days away from total breaking. 4 August 1939.

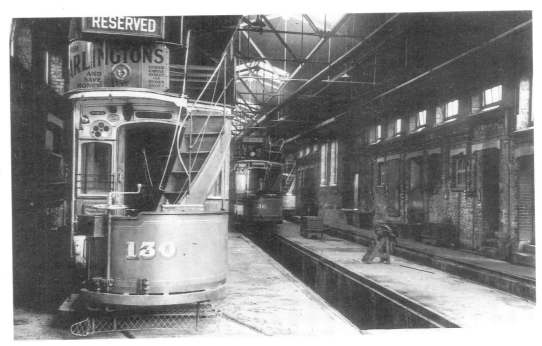

190) An inside view of Beaconsfield Road depot showing the tram pits and general gloom in which the cars were maintained. In shot left to right are cars 130, 36 and 135. 17 April 1939.

# PART 4

# THE GRAVEYARD

## AND

## MISCELLANEOUS ITEMS

# Old Market and Eastville Electric Tramways.

WEEK DAYS.—OLD MARKET TO EASTVILLE.

First cars depart at 5.50 a.m., 6.0, 6.55, 8.3, and then every few minutes until 11.30 p.m.

EASTVILLE TO OLD MARKET.

First cars depart at 5.25 a.m , 5.35, 6.30, 7.30, and then every few minutes until 10.48 p.m.

SUNDAYS.—Cars run every few minutes.

From EASTVILLE—First car 2 p.m., last 10 p.m.
From OLD MARKET—First car 2.45 p.m., last 10.30 p.m.

*Time occupied on journey.* To or from OLD MARKET and EASTVILLE, 12 minutes.

JOINT RAILWAY STATION.

Horse cars run every 10 minutes from 8 a.m. till 11 p.m. between OLD MARKET TERMINUS of the Electric Tramways and TOTTERDOWN, passing the JOINT RAILWAY STATION to and fro, the whole distance between the Station and Eastville occupying about 22 minutes.

## STOPPING PLACES.

Cars will not stop nor reduce speed to take up or set down passengers except at the Stopping Stations indicated by Rings painted around the trolley posts. Cars will stop only when required for passengers to alight or by intending passengers who wish to be taken up.

## DISTINGUISHING SIGNALS.

*The cars running to Eastville are distinguished by letter "E" over the canopy, and by Green Front Light at night.*

## ELECTRIC SIGNAL BELLS.

Electric Signal Bells are provided inside and outside for the use of passengers. When they wish the car stopped passengers should just before reaching a Stopping Station, ring the bell, and the Conductor will signal the Motorman to stop on arrival there.

TIME TABLES GIVING FULLER DETAILS ARE EXHIBITED ON THE CAR WINDOWS.

## FARE:

Old Market and Eastville (EITHER WAY)   -   -   -   -   -   Id.

191) In the 2nd batch was one of the Grinder cars (No.2) either ex car 86 or 97, but impossible to tell. Ironically in this, the last few days of its existence, this is one of the best photographs taken of the Grinder. Note the protection given the Driver which was not available to the passenger carrying vehicles. 4 August 1938.

192) Also in the 2nd batch was this row of vehicles being from left to right Nos. 6, 12, 28, 15 and 54, all to fall to the breakers hammer within 3 weeks of this photograph having been taken on the 4 August 1938.

193) Through the hole in the Wall car 57 stands out in the scrap yard ready for the axe to fall. Note the rails laid on wooden sleepers, the only time this occurred in Bristol and the house on the left of the tram shed. Workmen in background moving an electric motor. 4 August 1939.

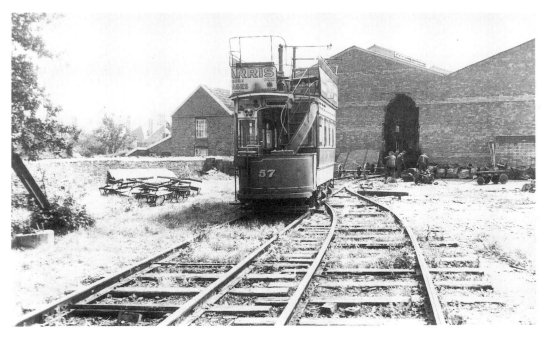

194) Another view of No.57 this time looking out into the yard from the shed. Around the curve in the track is car 118, minus the top deck seating and decency boards. Compare this and the previous picture of No. 57 which show the Harris Bacon corner advert carried by all trams at one end and the Regent petrol advert at the other. The two cars formed part of the 3rd batch of trams (50 in total) to be scrapped. 4 August 1939.

195) With the destination 'Arnos Vale' symbolically showing on car 138 there is a line up of 10 cars (6 in the photograph) thrown on the scrap heap and no longer required. Left to right in the view are Nos. 24, 138, 144, 181, 62 and 232. Behind are cars 13, 210, 47 and 183. 4 August 1939.

Not long after this picture was taken the last three trams in each row (24, 13, 210 and 135, 144 and 47) were retained on the siding as a War "Emergency Reserve" remaining there to the Spring of 1941.

196) At the opposite end of the above line of trams was the view on the right. Amongst the weeds is a lorry loaded with top deck seating taken from cars 118, 11, 1, 34 and 31. Also in shot are cars 58, 94, 109, 115, 212, 121, 78, 232, 62, 181, 144 and 138. 4 August 1939. (All these trams had been scrapped by 19 September 1939).

197) A view from the top deck showing a row of unidentified trams all lined up alongside Holly Hill and Alma Road and all considered redundant as Bristol raced to change over its public transport system to the Motor Bus. c.1938.

198) A close-up of the Trolley stand and arm plus the top deck seating arrangement. Note Mr. Challenger's patented hinged covers on the seats so as to keep the sitting area dry. Many of these seats ended up in local gardens and one is known to still exist in a local Doctor's surgery. c.1939.

199) Farewell Bristol trams, gone but not forgotten.

200) A view of Bedminster Depot not long after it had been built. 29 July 1901.

201) During the early evening of the 3rd January 1941 the Air Raid sirens sounded across Bristol and for the next 12 hours or so German aeroplanes continued to tear the heart out of the City. Towards the end of the raid around 6.00 a.m. on the 4th a large bomb struck the portals of the Bedminster Depot with the above effect. Cars 236, 87 and 136 caught by the blast stand isolated from the system they served so well.

202) All that remains of Car 71 which was on its way out of the Depot when the bomb fell killing the Driver. 4 January 1941.

203) Probably the remains of car 164 which like No.71 was totally destroyed by the bomb. 4 January 1941.

204) A close view of what is believed to be the remains of car 164. 4 January 1941.

205) The sorry state of what had been a graceful purpose-built building. The next journey of the unidentified car may well be Kingswood but not under its own power or with passengers. 4 January 1941.

206) Bedminster Depot in happier days with cars 223, 232 and 128 lined up with some of the depot staff and crew. 17 September 1938.

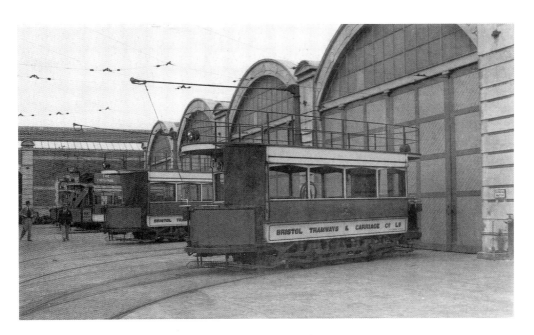

207) The two rail grinders standing in Brislington Depot yard around May 1938. Note the shortened platform and driver's protection sheet.

208) One of the special work's car employed by the Company to keep the track free from rubbish and/or snow, rests in the Staple Hill depot. 4 August 1938.

The Bristol Tramways & Carriage Company. Limited.

# NOTICE.

Passengers should REMAIN SEATED when the car is passing under RAILWAY BRIDGES, and are warned that it is dangerous to touch the Overhead Electric Wires.

Tramways Centre.
20th December, 1899.

CHAS. CHALLENGER.
*Traffic Manager*

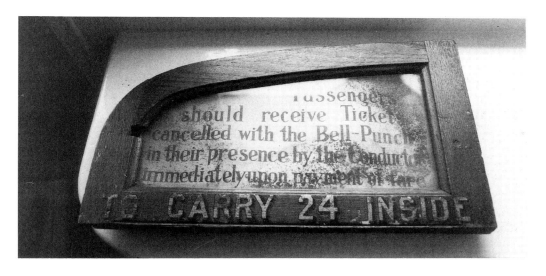

209) Part of Peter Davey's collection of tram ephemera, showing notices, plus a bell push and motor control handle from car 232.

210 & 211

Two signs saved from trams about to be scrapped in 1941.

Roller Blind showing various destinations.

All now part of Peter Davey's collection.

KINGSWOOD
ASHTON ROAD
BRISTOL BRIDGE
BEDMINSTER
DOWN
BEDMINSTER
DEPOT
KNOWLE
HANHAM
STAPLE HILL
7FTI ANN RD

NOTICES
PASSENGERS SHOULD REMAIN
SEATED WHEN THE TRAMCAR IS
PASSING UNDER RAILWAY BRIDGES
AND ARE WARNED THAT IT IS
DANGEROUS TO TOUCH THE
OVERHEAD ELECTRIC WIRES

DOGS ARE NOT ALLOWED INSIDE
ANY TRAMCAR, BUT AT THE
CONDUCTOR'S DISCRETION MAY
BE CARRIED ON THE UPPER DECK

THE BRISTOL TRAMWAYS & CARRIAGE CO., LTD

TURN
TROLLEY
THIS WAY

# THE FINAL DESTINATION

A potted history of the trams pictured in this book.

| Picture Number | Tram Car Number | Entered Service | Date Withdrawn | Remarks |
|---|---|---|---|---|
| 2 | 141 | 1899 | May 1938 | Originally built as the Directors Car in Shrewsbury. Rebuilt as a |
| 68 | | | | standard passenger tram in 1908. |
| 6/7 | 92 | 1895 | 1923 | When built at Birkenhead it had 3 side windows and was not as long as subsequent standard trams. |
| 8 | 94 | 1895 | Aug. 1939 | ditto (see also 136 and 196) |
| 11 | 89 | 1895 | Aug. 1939 | Same details as car 92, and can be seen in its re-built condition in pictures 64 and 153. |
| 16 | 199 | 1901 | July 1941 | Built in Shrewsbury |
| 17 | 198 | 1901 | Oct. 1938 | Built in Shrewsbury (see also 58/75). |
| 18 | 139 | 1898 | June 1939 | Built in Birkenhead |
| 22 | 192 | 1901 | July 1941 | Built in Shrewsbury. (see also 29/123/162) |
| | 194 | 1901 | June 1939 | Built in Shrewsbury. |
| 23 | 200 | 1901 | Oct. 1941 | Built in Shrewsbury. (see also 38/42/56/143) |
| 24 | 189 | 1901 | Aug. 1939 | Built in Shrewsbury (see also 85 and 184) |
| 28 | 121 | 1900 | Aug. 1939 | Built in Shrewsbury (see also 134). |
| 33 | 193 | 1901 | Sept. 1941 | Built in Shrewsbury |
| 37 | 124 | 1900 | June 1941 | Built in Shrewsbury (see also 53/181) |
| 41 | 150 | 1899 | June 1941 | Built in the USA by the American Car. Co. (see also 47) |
| 43 | 163 | 1900 | June 1941 | Built in Shrewsbury |
| 44 | 161 | 1899 | June 1941 | Built in America |
| | 88 | 1895 | Oct. 1938 | Built in Birkenhead |
| 46 | 135 | 1898 | June 1941 | Built in Birkenhead (see also 168/178/179) |
| 49 | 113 | 1900 | June 1941 | Built in Shrewsbury. (see also 73/143/150). This was the only tram taken out of the scrap line and put back into service, having been exchanged for car 125. |
| | 169 | 1900 | June 1941 | Built in Shrewsbury (see also 124/127). |
| 51 | 17 | 1900 | June 1941 | Built in Shrewsbury (see also 73/169) |
| 55 | 187 | 1900 | June 1941 | Built in Shrewsbury (see also 60/145 164/170) |
| 56 | 53 | 1900 | June 1941 | Built in Shrewsbury (see also 160) |
| 57 | 136 | 1898 | Feb 1941 | Built in Birkenhead (see also 201) |
| 59 | 34 | 1900 | Sept. 1939 | Built in Shrewsbury (see also 196) |
| 60 | 76 | 1900 | Nov. 1938 | Built in Shrewsbury. |
| 61 | 23 | 1900 | Sept. 1939 | Built in Shrewsbury (see also 62/140) |
| | 146 | 1899 | June 1938 | Built in America |
| | 174 | 1900 | Sept. 1938 | Built in Shrewsbury (see also 71/137/174) |
| 62 | 24 | 1900 | Mar. 1941 | Built in Shrewsbury (see also 85/145/195) |
| 63 | 122 | 1900 | Dec. 1938 | Built in Shrewsbury |
| | 160 | 1899 | May 1938 | Built in America |
| 64 | 126 | 1897 | June 1941 | Built in Birkenhead (see also 153/181) |
| | 188 | 1900 | June 1939 | Built in Shrewsbury (see also 134/146/153 and 182) |
| 65 | 18 | 1900 | Oct. 1938 | Built in Shrewsbury |
| 66 | 114 | 1900 | Oct. 1938 | Built in Shrewsbury (see also 77/138) |
| | 132 | 1897 | July 1941 | Built in Birkenhead (see 166/184) |
| | 158 | 1899 | Oct. 1941 | Built in America (see also 164). |
| | 197 | 1900 | Aug. 1941 | Built in Shrewsbury (see also 70) |
| 67 | 3 | 1900 | May 1938 | Built in Shrewsbury |
| | 118 | 1896 | Sept. 1939 | Built in Birkenhead (see also 143/194/196) |
| | 181 | 1900 | Sept. 1939 | Built in Shrewsbury. (see also 147/186/195) |
| 68 | 164 | 1900 | Jan. 1941 | Built in Shrewsbury. This car was destroyed by enemy action. (see also 181/203). |
| 69 | 166 | 1900 | Feb. 1941 | Built in Shrewsbury. Badly damaged by enemy action. |
| 71 | 29 | 1900 | June 1941 | Built in Shrewsbury. |
| 72 | 152 | 1899 | July 1939 | Built in America (see 73/90) |
| 73 | 75 | 1899 | Oct. 1938 | Built in Shrewsbury |
| 74 | 112 | 1899 | April 1941 | Built in Shrewsbury |
| 84 | 227 | 1901 | Jan. 1941 | Built in Shrewsbury (see also 130) |
| 87 | 208 | 1901 | May 1938 | Built in Shrewsbury (see also 111) |
| 88 | 207 | 1901 | Sept. 1938 | Built in Shrewsbury (see also 125). |
| 89 | 204 | 1901 | Oct. 1938 | Built in Shrewsbury |

| Picture Number | Tram Car Number | Entered Service | Date Withdrawn | Remarks |
|---|---|---|---|---|
| 90 | 68 | 1900 | June 1938 | Built in Shrewsbury (see also 97) |
| 97 | 72 | 1900 | Dec. 1938 | Built in Shrewsbury |
| 98 | 67 | 1900 | June 1941 | Built in Shrewsbury |
| 99 | 71 | 1900 | Jan. 1941 | Built in Shrewsbury. Destroyed by enemy action. (see also 202) |
|  | 157 | 1899 | June 1941 | Built in America. (See also 167) |
| 100 | 10 | 1900 | May 1938 | Built in Shrewsbury |
| 101 | 80 | 1900 | Nov. 1938 | Built in Shrewsbury |
| 104 | 120 | 1900 | May 1938 | Built in Shrewsbury |
| 105 | 73 | 1900 | Sept. 1938 | Built in Shrewsbury (see also 113/124). |
| 108 | 69 | 1900 | Nov. 1938 | Built in Shrewsbury |
| 109 | 70 | 1900 | July 1941 | Built in Shrewsbury (see also 119/123) |
| 110 | 131 | 1897 | July 1941 | Built in Birkenhead. |
| 112 | 72 | 1900 | Dec. 1938 | Built in Shrewsbury |
| 114 | 133 | 1897 | July 1939 | Built in Birkenhead (see also 128) |
| 115 | 214 | 1901 | Mar. 1941 | Built in Shrewsbury |
| 121 | 85 | 1900 | Oct. 1938 | Built in Shrewsbury |
| 122 | 48 | 1900 | Dec. 1938 | Built in Shrewsbury |
| 129 | 232 | 1901 | Sept. 1939 | Built in Shrewsbury (see also 195) |
| 130 | 82 | 1900 | Oct. 1938 | Built in Shrewsbury |
|  | 145 | 1899 | May 1938 | Built in America |
| 133 | 129 | 1897 | Sept. 1938 | Built in Birkenhead |
| 134 | 38 | 1900 | Aug. 1938 | Built in Shrewsbury |
| 135 | 7 | 1900 | Sept. 1941 | Built in Shrewsbury (see also 171) |
|  | 224 | 1901 | Sept. 1941 | Built in Shrewsbury |
|  | 227 | 1901 | Jan. 1941 | Built in Shrewsbury |
| 136 | 211 | 1901 | Sept. 1938 | Built in Shrewsbury |
| 139 | 172 | 1900 | Nov. 1938 | Built in Shrewsbury (see also 186) |
| 141 | 19 | 1900 | June 1941 | Built in Shrewsbury (see also 188) |
| 143 | 182 | 1900 | Oct. 1938 | Built in Shrewsbury (see also 186) |
|  | 137 | 1898 | Oct. 1938 | Built in Birkenhead |
| 144 | 116 | 1895 | 1923 | Built in Birkenhead |
| 145 | 36 | 1900 | Sept. 1941 | Built in Shrewsbury (see also 169/190) |
| 149 | 216 | 1901 | Aug. 1941 | Built in Shrewsbury (see also 149/185/188) |
| 150 | 236 | 1920 | Feb. 1941 | Built at Brislington (see also 201) |
| 152 | 14 | 1900 | June 1939 | Built in Shrewsbury |
|  | 143 | 1899 | July 1941 | Built in America |
| 157 | 12 | 1900 | Aug. 1938 | Built in Shrewsbury (see also 192) |
| 158 | 196 | 1900 | Oct. 1938 | Built in Shrewsbury |
| 180 | 86 | 1920 | Aug. 1941 | Built at Brislington |
| 182 | 33 | 1900 | Aug. 1939 | Built in Shrewsbury (see also 189) |
| 183 | 171 | 1900 | Sept. 1941 | Built in Shrewsbury |
| 185 | 173 | 1900 | Sept. 1941 | Built in Shrewsbury |
| 186 | 170 | 1900 | Sept. 1938 | Built in Shrewsbury |
|  | 183 | 1900 | Sept. 1939 | Built in Shrewsbury |
| 192 | 6 | 1900 | Aug. 1938 | Built in Shrewsbury |
|  | 28 | 1900 | Aug. 1938 | Built in Shrewsbury (see also 192) |
|  | 15 | 1900 | Aug. 1938 | Built in Shrewsbury |
|  | 54 | 1900 | Aug. 1938 | Built in Shrewsbury |
| 193 | 57 | 1900 | Aug. 1939 | Built in Shrewsbury (see also 194) |
| 195 | 138 | 1898 | April 1941 | Built in Birkenhead |
|  | 144 | 1899 | April 1941 | Built in America |
|  | 62 | 1900 | Sept. 1939 | Built in Shrewsbury |
| 196 | 11 | 1900 | Aug. 1939 | Built in Shrewsbury |
|  | 1 | 1900 | Sept. 1939 | Built in Shrewsbury |
|  | 31 | 1900 | Aug. 1939 | Built in Shrewsbury |
|  | 58 | 1900 | Aug. 1939 | Built in Shrewsbury |
|  | 109 | 1900 | Aug. 1939 | Built in Shrewsbury |
|  | 115 | 1900 | Sept. 1939 | Built in Shrewsbury |
|  | 212 | 1901 | Sept. 1939 | Built in Shrewsbury |
| 201 | 87 | 1895 | April 1941 | Built in Birkenhead |

Of the 237 trams which plied the streets of Bristol during the first forty years of this century, no less than 115 are depicted in this book.